A B+ Life

A B+ Life

ELIZABETH RICISAK

Charleston, SC
www.PalmettoPublishing.com

A B+ Life
Copyright © 2023 by Elizabeth Ricisak

First Edition

Paperback: 979-8-8229-2539-7
eBook: 979-8-8229-2540-3

Dedication

To my precious husband, who reminds me daily,
that in his eyes, I have always been an A+.

To my two children who accompanied me throughout much of this
difficult journey. Their childhoods were anything but conventional,
yet they grew to be exceptional adults in every area of their lives.
I couldn't be prouder, more grateful, or love them more.

*Note: The cover of this book was done by a very special young man named Tim McHugh. Although Tim was born on-the-spectrum, in his 30+ years he has mastered language, works a full-time job, attends college, and is a self-taught artist. I wanted to showcase Tim's incredible talent on my book cover. It is my hope that others will use Tim's extraordinary artistic talent for future projects. His email: tim.timmchugh.mchugh@gmail.com

Chapter One

I WAS NOT BORN INTO MONEY, FAME, OR INTELLECT. IN FACT, my childhood was nothing special. Actually, it was truly less than special. I was a plain girl from a plain house. My father worked in a warehouse during the week. On Saturdays he delivered flowers for a small florist shop. He would come home cussing because he drove all over the city to deliver the flowers yet had to turn in his tips. He earned $3 an hour. Saturday nights were never happy because he came home exhausted and frustrated. On Sundays, he worked in a small butcher shop. He'd bring the meat home that was too brown to sell but could still be cooked. I grew up thinking that meat was supposed to have an "off" odor before it was cooked. Perhaps that's why I am a moderate vegetarian. He also got to keep all the dented cans of vegetables and soups. I can still see my parents having to open the cans with garage tools because the can opener would not work on the dents.

During the work week, supper (I didn't know the word dinner) was always at 5:00pm because Dad's shift ended at four and he'd come home exhausted and famished. He'd walk in with his tin lunch box and empty coffee thermos, dropping them on the counter, and sit down to eat. Mom would remove the wax paper and lay it out straight so she could get another day out of it. Potatoes were in every meal. Rice was not a food to my dad. White bread and a jar of jelly were staples on the table. White milk and black coffee for every meal.

Since the kitchen was small, we had a booth for the three kids to share and my parents each had their own chairs. My youngest brother, who was either dyslexic, extremely ADHD, or just plain bad, made life tough. He would ruin almost every meal with his lack of manners. To teach him how to eat properly, my dad would reach across the table and smack his knuckles with his fork until he acted accordingly. There were many a bloody knuckle in my childhood. I used to hate supper time. There was never any engaging conversation.

My mother stayed home. She washed clothes on Mondays which were hung on the outside clothesline no matter what season it was. It wasn't until I started doing my own laundry in college that I realized you are not supposed to use the same water for all of the loads of laundry. My mother used the same water for each load. I suppose this was because she worried so much about their lack of money. Also, I did not know until much later in my life that soot was not a natural phenomenon. Being raised in a steel town during the heyday of steel production, I assumed that all clothes would have soot to shake off after being dried on the line and all the car windows would be cleaned each morning.

Mom ironed on Tuesday. I mean, she ironed *all* day on Tuesday. That included pillowcases, dad's handkerchiefs, underwear, and clothes. I can remember Mom hating ironing day so much that she scrounged together coins out of the bottom of the junk drawer or her purse to send me to the bakery down the hill. She told me to buy as many secondhand goodies as possible. Of course, it took me years to re-alize that she meant day-old baked goods. It was the only thing that got her through her ironing day. She nibbled on those day-old donuts or cakes I'd bring home. Even though my mom was not the most emotionally stable person, she had a funny sense of humor. She would always say that when she died, she knew she'd go to heaven, but she just knew that she'd get the job of ironing the damn angel outfits. To this day, I smile every time I see a nativity scene with beautiful angels wearing glorious white gowns.

Wednesday was cleaning day, or as we called it, "red-up day." I later learned that was a slang term borrowed from the Pennsylvania Dutch, who used to say they were going to ready up the house for guests. Who knew? I often find myself, 60 years later, telling my husband that I'm busy "redding-up" the house. It just works for me.

Thursday was window washing. I remember standing on a ladder outside, washing the second story window as a young teen when I got my first menstrual period. I had no idea what was happening, such things were not talked about back then. All I knew was something was gushing down my leg, and it was not the bucket of dirty water. To this day, I associate washing windows with depression and pain. I'd rather cash in my wine money to hire someone to wash my windows than do it myself.

Friday was shopping. Shopping consisted of the local supermarket for boxes of processed foods and cans of overcooked vegetables. If there was money left over, Mom would buy Braunschweiger, Limburger cheese, and sardines to please Dad when he wanted a snack at night drinking beer. I have never been able to stomach any of those delicacies. I couldn't even be in the same room.

Lastly, we always stopped at the beer distributor for Dad's beer. There was always money for beer. It was my morning chore to take his empty beer bottles to the garage and put them in the beer carton so he could return them each Friday. I never dared forget to do my chore. You see, Friday was when my dad got paid, so that's the day Mom could shop. The problem was my dad never wanted her to learn to drive. So, she couldn't go anywhere without him taking her. Finally, she got up the nerve to ask him to teach her to drive. That experience will haunt me forever. The three of us kids had to sit in the back seat of an old Buick while he tried to teach her to drive. We would wail when we had to go. Most of the teaching was yelling and tears. It would always end with frustration and anger. I used to wonder if my mom was just not bright, because she made so many mistakes trying to drive the car. However, as I look back, the poor woman must have been terrified.

We went to a Catholic school as kids. It was across the railroad tracks, literally. It was not in a neighborhood that I knew, but we were assigned to that school and church through the diocese, so we had no choice, and it would have been a sin to question the church. My mother, a devout Catholic, would never question what the diocese assigned. Not knowing any of the kids and not living near them did not promote friendships for any of us. I remember having forty kids in my classroom run by one old nun who was not a trained teacher. I did well though, because of my need to please. But I did not have any friends. I just smiled and went through each day secretly daydreaming of being the May Queen. That's every Catholic girl's dream.

However, my younger brother ruined my dream. He would be spanked almost daily in the principal's office. Every time he got into trouble, I would be called to the office to be told what he did and what to tell my mother when I got home. I was always the messenger. This made me so angry with my brother and even more angry with the nuns.

As I have said before and totally believe to be true, there are no coincidences in life. Each piece of the puzzle comes together with time. Ironically, I would grow up to become a teacher with an M.Ed in Reading. It was only then that I realized just how dyslexic my younger brother was. That poor kid couldn't read. Instead of someone understanding his disability, he was beaten for misbehaving and disobeying the nuns. Almost sixty years later, this man is one of the most successful men I know. He has always struggled with language, written and spoken. However, he overcame his disability by using his natural, engaging personality and wit. But in the meantime, he got the three of us thrown out of the Catholic school that year. He only made it to 2nd grade, me to 4th grade, and my older brother to 6th grade.

Attending a public school and the idea of being allowed to wear pants to school without hearing any religious mumbo jumbo was a shock. But truly the most challenging part for me was never having experienced a physical education class. I am still mortified that I started 5th grade, and I couldn't do a somersault or a cartwheel. Everyone stared at me as I tried. I think the public-school kids thought I was physically disabled. There was no time in Catholic school for any physical nonsense. From that day forward, PE would never be my friend.

Mom was not a healthy role model for me. I am sorry to be so blunt with that realization. She was emotionally immature, needy, and generally depressed. Perhaps it was because she was the youngest of ten Irish siblings. By the time she was born, her mom was forty-six years old and had nine other children. Her father was an Irish immigrant with a severe drinking problem. I'm sure she lacked the parenting she needed and didn't have a great role model either. I do remember one thing though: she named me after her mom. She told me all of my life that her mother was a saint, and I must always live up to her name. Perhaps this message has resonated with me throughout my life, forcing me to try hard to be a saint. Whatever that meant.

I spent most of my childhood trying to keep Mom happy. I was sandwiched between two brothers who were neither remarkable nor kind to me. My mother could not control or discipline them, so I learned at a very early age that it would behoove me to distract the boys in order to keep them from upsetting my mother. There were winter nights, when Dad was bowling, that she'd walk out the door to get away from their misbehavior. That left me in charge, and I was certainly not equipped for the task. I think I was seventeen years old before I went directly to bed without having to read them to sleep. I learned that if I read to them, they would not fight with each other. Then my mom wouldn't go out into the night to walk down the street. When my dad was home, if I read to them, I would prevent my dad from flying up the stairs to beat them. That would prevent my mother going into an emotional breakdown. So, it was just what I had to do. It all relied on me to keep the peace. I can clearly remember the first time I went to my tiny bedroom at age seventeen, when the boys were gone, and I could fall asleep at my own pace. I would only learn years later that no friend of mine had ever had to do this as a child. I had believed this was normal behavior as the peacemaker.

My dad was a first-generation German. I can say that I do believe he loved me, although he never hugged or kissed me. He was uneducated, cold, and not overly excited about being a dad. I think he came back from the Korean War and decided that he should marry and have kids. No thought was put forth, it just happened. I used to dream that my parents had a fairytale love story. However, if their love was a fairytale, I no longer wanted to be a princess. His parents were old Germans who showed no love for him or for each other. He knew what he knew, and it was not a gentle hand, just like his cruel father.

I may have been my dad's favorite. However, I have to admit, the competition was not too tough. My older brother, who was eighteen months older, was an unhappy kid: I was never sure why. I just believe he, too, was born into the wrong family. I believe he felt alone, and misunderstood. My younger brother, eighteen months younger, was always into making mischief. He didn't seem to care about the outcome of his actions. Yet he was clever enough and knew how to manipulate my parents, and it usually worked, which only angered my older brother further.

Dad used corporal punishment as his discipline. He broke a few arms on my brothers, as well as some pretty rough bruises. I never faulted him for it though. My brothers constantly taunted him by fighting in their bedroom directly above where he sat to watch television. Why didn't they just behave? It seemed so simple to me. How did they not understand the simple concept of cause and effect? Dad would come flying up those steps swinging at them almost every night. I knew little about good parenting at that point, mainly because I hadn't experienced it. So, I prayed on the hard floor every night that they would start to be sweet and submissive so as not to upset Dad. I believed that if I prayed hard enough, and my knees hurt enough, my prayers would be answered. Sadly, the prayers were never answered. Although Dad was naturally an easy-going guy, his temper was my biggest fear. As a sexist man, he would never hit me because he believed girls were weak and fragile. Not to appear angelic, however, I really tried hard to please my dad. I don't think I ever disappointed him when I was young.

But it was not unlike him to fight with my mother, often ending evening meals by throwing dishes in the sink. Both my parents were stubborn and strong-willed, so this was a weekly occurrence and a recipe for unhappiness. I secretly made a promise that if and when I ever married, I would never fight like this in front of my kids. It terrified me. In fact, I grew to especially hate Sundays because of the boredom, exhaustion, rotten weather, and the never-ending worry about money that inevitably led to a fight. I had a secret place in the woods that I can still see as clearly as ever, fifty-plus years later, where I would run to hide. I would stay there as long as I could before having to return home. By the time I returned home, the TV would be blaring, and Dad would be drinking his Iron City beer with Mom dozing in the chair. It would be safe until bedtime. Then I'd do my reading thing to keep the boys quiet.

I can remember crossing the woods to the nicer neighborhood to visit friends from school. When I think of kids today, there is no way they would have crossed dark woods, jumped over creeks, and over busy roads to visit friends. No parent would allow that today. Back then, if I wanted to have any friends, I had to get to them the best way I knew. No one really knew where I was half the time, as long as I was home for supper. It always shocked me when I visited their houses. They had regularly scheduled lunchtimes on weekends, where their moms would actually make lunch. Up to that point, I assumed there were two meals in each day, and you were on your own at home between breakfast and dinner. Their homes were fancy, calm, and quiet. No one was fighting or yelling. They had snacks in their pantry. In fact, they actually had a pantry, an entire closet to hold endless amounts of goodies. I was always in awe of how good they had it.

Note to self: You can't always get what you want, but if you try sometime, you'll find you get what you need... (Mick Jagger)

Chapter Two

MY MOM TRIED. ON OUR BIRTHDAYS SHE WOULD MAKE A BOX cake and we'd get to choose the dinner menu. Unfortunately, I was born in January, after Christmas, so there was never any money for a birthday gift. She always felt bad for me, so she would sneak a quarter on my birthday every year to buy an ice cream bar after lunch at school. I waited all year for that ice cream bar. I ate it slowly, with the biggest smile on my face.

Mom just wasn't emotionally strong. I believe she truly suffered from Seasonal Affective Disorder in addition to massive insecurity. She was short and heavy. I think she could have been pretty, if she wasn't heavy, but she never really tried. So, it was hard to tell. However, my giving heart came from her. She was naturally kind. Her finest quality was her pleasure to give. She'd be the neighbor that would go door to door to collect pennies for a sick neighbor or a family in need. It was just what she did. I will forever be grateful that she taught me how to give and be of service to others. But there was always one twist to her kindness. She had an insatiable need to be recognized and thanked for every kind thing she did. It took years for me to realize that the act of giving and helping is to be done for the sake of others, not for the sake of making oneself feel acknowledged. There is a huge difference. I made it my life's work to serve others without wanting or needing recognition.

The most terrifying time with my mother was when I was left alone with her. My brothers would be out, my dad would be at work. This happened enough to almost destroy my childhood. I tried so hard to prevent her wrath by cleaning. I'd wake up extra early and clean before she got up. My thought was if she woke up to see the floors scrubbed, the toilets cleaned, and the house organized, then she'd be happy. But it never seemed to work out the way I planned, no matter how hard I tried. I now know that she viewed me as her scapegoat. She had no one else. I guess it's true; we tend to hurt the person who loves us the most.

The dining room was tiny. There was a table in the center with a few chairs along the walls. She would start to cry about her horrible, difficult life. Then she would scream about my cruel dad. Then her eyes would get huge, and she'd start to shake. She'd chase me around the table, screaming like a mad woman. I would be terrified. I'd beg her to stop. But she was not herself. She didn't look like herself. She was a wild beast. Finally, I would fall to the floor begging her to stop. I promised over and over again that I would try to be a better little girl if she would just stop screaming. I sobbed and sobbed. Finally, after what seemed like hours, she would be exhausted and quit.

Eventually, hours later, she would come to me to hold me, asking for forgiveness, saying that I'm the only one she has to talk to about her problems. For the rest of the day, she would be very maternal to me, almost to say she was sorry. But I knew it would happen again and again, and as a little girl, I believed it was my sole responsibility to take the wrath in order to keep my mom sane and alive. To this day, neither of my brothers or my dad ever knew that this occurred.

I'm now in my sixties. I have never been fat. There's a reason. I will starve myself if I even think I looked fat. I know that is because I was so traumatized by my mom's lack of self-control concerning her diet and her personal hygiene. My dad asked her often to lose weight. The truth is, I felt bad for her because she would cry and cry to me about her weight. I was angry at my dad for years for picking on her.

However, as I got older, I noticed that she just would not stop eating. Like many closet eaters, no one actually sees the eating happening. Her portions at mealtime were moderate. That's why she'd cry, saying it wasn't fair. But what I observed was that mom ate as she cooked. She'd eat a large portion while she was cooking or baking. She loved to make chocolate chip cookies to give away, but the truth is, she consumed most of them.

There was a time when I was consoling her about a dress she was to wear to a function. My job was to tell her how pretty she looked. In fact, years later, my bridesmaid at my wedding reminded me that when we went shopping for my wedding dress, we spent the day finding the perfect dress for her, not me. I truly didn't mind. Her happiness provided me with peace.

I knew what to say to make her feel better. I had done it a million times before. However, this particular time, Mom undressed in front of me. It was just her and me. I had never seen a naked obese person. I was traumatized to the extent that I can still see her to this day. It was at that moment that I was no longer angry with my dad for nagging about her weight. I can't begin to understand how he could sleep with her. From that day forward, I have been obsessed about my figure. Her stretch pants that women used to wear back then were all fuzzy near the crotch. That's because her legs rubbed together all the time. In my crazy perception, I still see fat when I look at my thighs. The image will haunt me forever. I've punished myself often for these thoughts, but I loathe that image embedded in my memory.

I believed that I was not a pretty child. I was the kid who got out of a swimming pool and did not look pretty. I had friends whose hair looked lovely when wet or whose eyes had long lashes that were accentuated when wet. Not me. I just did not do "wet" well. In fact, at a much later age, I lived in paradise and still refused to swim in public. My darling husband has tried to help me, but the pain is deep. I've always believed that I was homely when wet. I'd never had those movie-star looks like other girls.

So, at a really young age, I decided to capitalize on my secret weapon that I was given. I had been given an amazing ability to get along with anyone. My friends teased me that I was born with "the happy gene." Basically, that means that my default mood was always pleasant and positive, unlike those who wake up grumpy or see the glass half empty in all situations. I was usually smiling. Everyone liked me, everyone was my friend. I was nice to the boys who no other girls noticed. I was good to old people, babies, and teachers. I loved anyone, especially the underdogs. I simply saw life as a happy experience, for the most part. Therefore, I used my talent with building relationships to create a personality that would take me places. I remember believing with all of my heart that I didn't mind not being beautiful because it made me develop other more important areas in my life. The truly gorgeous girls never had to try hard because everyone doted on them all the time. Therefore, I used my wit, heart, and intellect to get ahead.

The best way to describe my self-image was believing I was a B+ girl. In school, receiving a B+ is good. It's not great, but it is good. I was not brilliant but determined enough to appear bright. I was not beautiful but learned the tricks of hair style and make-up that made me appear attractive. I wasn't overly athletic but had such a creative mind that I made it onto teams with my creative try-out performances. I didn't have boyfriends who wanted to date me but was voted as the sweetest girl in the school. Most things I did, I did well-perhaps not to a mastery level, but at least a B+.

I was satisfied with what I was and how things were going in high school until the day there was a vote for the ten most beautiful girls in the senior class. (What a cruel tradition!) Neither talent nor grades had anything to do with the contest; it was strictly based on physical appearance. At that time, I was on an elite dance team. It was very difficult to make the team and I was not a dancer. Most of the girls who made the team had had years of dancing lessons. That was not my case. My parents could not afford for me to have any extracurricular lessons. But I always created such cute auditions that I made the team three years running. Our neighbors used to tease my parents that they watched me practice my creative audition so much that they knew it. They laughed saying that if I did not make it, they would perform it for me to get me on the team. My determination, not my talent, always worked for me.

Again, it was my personality and creativity that got me through. The team's uniforms were short skirts and high boots. The prettiest, most popular girls clamored to be part of this team. Of course, the drill team would probably comprise all of the girls who would make that elite top ten beauty list. So, on the day that the entire senior class of 1,200 students voted on the ten prettiest girls, it turned out to be the black hole of my teen years. That night, the ten winners were given a phone call to let them know they were chosen. Of course, my phone didn't ring.

But because I was so popular, all ten winners called me, excited to tell me they were chosen, assuming that I would have been one of the ten. I think they thought since I was so nice that my beauty would shine through. It doesn't work that way. I wasn't on that list. But I jumped up and down with enthusiastic congratulations for each phone call, listening intently about the details of their photography session for the yearbook post.

That night, I cried myself to sleep. No, I sobbed myself to sleep. It was the first time that I really believed that I have never and will never be a pretty woman. I believed that I was just not good enough. It was that horrible night crying myself to sleep that I resolved if I ever had a daughter of my own, she would *not* be taught to focus on physical looks. She would be smart, strong, and successful. She would never value looks enough to have her world shattered by a stupid vote. Those girls were all A girls. I was still only a B+. My dad used to say, "Lizzie, you're as ugly as a mud fence!" And I thought all those years that he had been kidding. Maybe there is always a small amount of truthfulness in kidding.

Note to self: As a teacher and a mother, I will do everything I can to prevent little girls from believing that their life success is based on a pretty face and shapely body.

Chapter Three

WHEN YOU ARE NOT FORTUNATE TO BE RAISED BY COLLEGE-ED-ucated parents, there is a real disadvantage of knowing what to do when it's time to think about college. My parents preached to the three of us that we would go to college, no matter what! They collected Savings Bonds and War Bonds for years to pay for our tuition when the time came. I had no idea how they scrimped to buy bonds for us. But even though I had tuition money, I was totally unprepared for the task at hand. I had no relatives to ask. I really didn't understand the college process at all. I literally chose a college because my friends chose it. I literally chose a major because I heard it was easy and I was terrified to not be able to get through college. I didn't know anything about how to apply or what needed to be done. I just followed my friends and landed where they landed.

Many years later, after retiring from thirty-five years of teaching school, everyone assumes it was my life's dream to teach. Quite the contrary; I had never given it a thought. I chose it because I was told that elementary education was so easy, no one had ever failed. My fear of not being good enough made my decision for me. I would choose a major where I would pass. The truth of the matter, I do believe in my heart that it was not an accident that I studied education. Fate took over when I needed guidance and had none. It turned out to be a perfect profession for this caregiving, people-pleasing, sunny, wide-eyed, B+ girl. I think God had his hand in it even if I was clueless at the time.

College was a continuation of high school. I was popular and had a lot of fun. But I had to learn how to study and keep my grades acceptable. Freshman year was not easy for me. I did not have the necessary academic skills. But one thing I had was discipline. I tried, and I kept trying. I worked very hard.

I was immature and certainly not worldly. I lived with a girl who went crazy as soon as her parents drove off campus. She never went to class and was high most of the time. I wasn't getting the support that I needed, but I kept myself on track. My high school friends whom I had followed were quieter and hung together with not a lot of branching. I was bored with their lack of adventure. I felt that I needed to move on and grow. I decided that joining a sorority was the way to blossom.

Looking back on it, I disagree with almost every aspect of my sorority life. Of course, the one I decided to join chose their members mainly on beauty and personality. It was joining the drill team all over again. I now so clearly see how our behavioral patterns continue throughout our lives. I was recreating my high school situation. How I wished I had chosen a different course. Why couldn't I have hung with the down-to-earth dorm residents or joined a club that fostered some charitable cause? We tend to make the same mistakes over and over. Don't get me wrong; I made lifelong friends whom I adore to this day. We love each other dearly. But even after many, many years, when we have our sorority reunions, I still feel like much of our conversations are superficial discussing recipes, cooking, gardening, yoga, house décor and illness. I have never felt that our conversations focused on the gifts of the soul, which is my true treasure. So, most of the time, during these gatherings, I would sit silently listening to the chatter, laughing at the silliness, and wondering if anyone else anywhere, viewed the world as I did.

I think I was the only freshman who went off to school knowing nothing about how sex worked. I had been raised Catholic by my Irish mother. She was a devout Catholic and talking about sex to me would have been a sin in her eyes. In my house for eighteen years, I had never seen my two brothers or my dad in their underwear. My dad would have died before he would even consider the subject, let alone kiss my mother on the cheek in front of me. It was such an uptight environment. I went to college truly not know anything concerning this subject.

One winter night during the first couple of months at college, I found out about a sex-education lecture being given in the basement of another dorm. I attended without telling anyone. I was so embarrassed. I wore a hooded sweatshirt and sat in the back. How angry I was after that lecture. I was so ill prepared to be on my own. How could my parents have sent me off alone without such pertinent information? If I wasn't such a cautious kid, I could have gotten myself in a whole lot of unknown danger. After that evening, I would never look at a boy the same again. How pathetic to be nineteen and find out how it all works. All I could think about was if I ever had a daughter, she would be educated and confident in her sexuality.

Being from a strict catholic background, I knew that I could never engage in sex until I married anyway. So, I felt slightly better about not worrying about it. However, a state university is a sex bowl! How does one avoid it? My sorority roommates were all sexually active. I held tough. No way. In fact, I had never even learned how to use a tampon. How could I possibly understand how anything longer and thicker could actually fit? So, all my dates were left at the door with nothing more than some heavy kissing. I can clearly admit that I did not make the connection between kissing them and feeling them growing as we kissed. They must have been so frustrated with me.

Finally, I met a grad student the end of my junior year when I was twenty-one years old. His name was Peter. (Of course, he was appropriately named "Peter.") He was crazy about me, but my heart was not into it. However, we were great friends and he made me laugh. I confided in him that I had never had sex and after twenty-one years I was beginning to wonder if I ever could. I was thinking I would be the one girl who couldn't have sex for some reason. This is the power of a Catholic upbringing. The guilt is relentless and unforgiving. So just to think about something taboo makes you feel like it is a sin.

On a side note, this was the very moment in my life that I realized the unhealthy power that Catholicism has on its followers. This was the beginning of the end of following the Catholic Church for me. I had been fed a whole lot of misinformation and I now had to deal with my uneasiness and anger concerning what I believed to be true. I have known many incredible Catholics who do such good. But this religion will never be what I believe to be my true path to spirituality, and I must let it go.

So, guess what I did? Yep. I asked Peter to teach me how to have sex. I explained that I just wanted him to walk me through the process step by step. Forty-plus years later I can still see his face, not unlike the face of someone who has just learned that he's holding a winning lottery ticket. I didn't understand his face at the time, as all I wanted was a clinical experience.

One thing I was good at was choosing great guy friends. Guys are not complicated creatures, and since sex had never been a concern for me, I had a lot of platonic guy friends. Guys just want to laugh and hang out. Being with guys gave me a reprieve from the standards of what I had to live up to with my sorority friends. Peter was a perfect guy friend.

On the night we agreed to do this experiment, I went to Peter's apartment. He shared it with three other guys, but mysteriously, no one was there but Peter. I entered the room. The living room was surrounded by flickering candles. There were rose petals on the floor and a mattress in the middle of the room, beautifully arranged. Music was playing. It was quite a lovely scene. How sweet of him.

But...the next hour was one of the worst experiences of my life. No one ever told me how painful it was. I cried. I bled. I stopped. I decided at that moment that I would never have sex again. I was the one and only girl on the planet that just could *not* do it. Perhaps I should reconsider my Catholicism and become a nun. I was not joking. At twenty-one years old, I needed to rethink my plan. Poor Peter...was petered out.

Note to self: A hearty bowel movement is ten times more satisfying than sex...concluded the disgruntled virgin.

Chapter Four

IT WAS IN COLLEGE THAT I FELL IN LOVE FOR THE FIRST TIME. I mean, head over heels in love. I had a boyfriend my senior year in high school, who was a true gem. He was perfect. But that was puppy love. Turns out I should have hung on to that sweet guy, for he went on to have a very successful life. To his credit, he remained a constant friend to me throughout my life. Even if I hurt him all those years ago, our friendship had weathered the storms of life, and he will always remain special in my heart.

At nineteen years old, I did not have a lot of experience, especially when it came to understanding true infatuation. So it was in college, that I fell crazy hard, head over heels, for a football player. Interestingly enough, like good wine, I had blossomed in college. Because of my pretty face and cute figure, this big man on campus took notice of me. We dated. We went to formals. I was never so happy. But there is a very thin line between euphoric happiness and heartbreak. He crushed me. But, like every pathetic love novice, I forgave him and took him back. In fact, more times than I can count. Until a person feels a true heartbreak over a lost love, it is difficult to put into words the extent of the ache. You'd do anything to fix it. I now believe that as much as I don't wish this heartache on anyone, we should all experience a broken heart at least once. Because inevitably you will be the heartbreaker someday. You have to know how bad it feels to crush someone's dream, to bring a person to their knees. Empathy is a necessity when it comes to the business of love.

This guy would swoop into my life off and on for three years. I would take anything he would offer, a movie, a phone call, a drive. It didn't matter, because I was that crazy about him. Finally, I'd had enough of being disappointed. After college graduation, I gave up hope on him. Then my life took a dramatic change. I had graduated early in three and a half years. It was January of my senior year; I was offered a teaching job at twenty-one years old. I moved into an apartment in a small country town with my best friend. It was a mountain town in Western Pennsylvania. Truly a beautiful place. My best friend was doing her student teaching while I was beginning my teaching career. It was a perfect time. My career began and I was ecstatic.

Everything was going as planned until one Friday afternoon in March. My roommate and I were planning to head to downtown Pittsburgh to meet our sorority sisters for a fun weekend. I was driving on my way home from school when I hit black ice. It was March 21, 1980. I hit that invisible ice and did everything you should *not* do when you skid on ice. This caused me to collide head-on with a coal truck coming down the mountain. This moment changed my life forever. I was knocked unconscious and thrown from my car. Of course, I wasn't wearing a seatbelt back then. My purse was damaged in the car's wreckage. Therefore, when the paramedics came, they could not identify me. It wasn't until a passing car stopped with children in it who recognized their teacher lying on the road. Again, not a coincidence: I later learned from the parent of those children that they decided to go a different route home and came upon my accident. They'd never used that particular road before. They were able to identify me. Over my lifetime I will be reminded many times of God's divine intervention.

My parents were two hours away. By the time they got to the hospital with my younger brother, I was in serious shape. I had a broken left arm, a broken left ankle, a broken right foot, broken cheekbones, and a fractured skull. My brother walked into the ER and fainted. My parents had to be sedated. Nothing would ever be the same.

I was in a country hospital. Since I was fortunate not to have internal damage, they left me there. But that meant my parents had to drive each day. My mother cried too much. My dad yelled at her for crying. I could do nothing to remedy the situation. I was trapped in a broken body and a bed where they kept me highly sedated. When I finally understood what had happened, it was several days later.

In the meantime, my parents moved all of my stuff out of my apartment and took it home. That left my roommate to fend on her own. She could not afford the place on her own. She was very upset with me for a long time that I screwed up her life, especially during her student teaching. I would loyally defend her when my mother would tell me that she didn't care about my accident, she only cared about her inconvenience. It would take me years later to understand that maybe my mother had been correct. The deep friendship that I honored was nothing more than superficial. However, she managed to get through her student teaching, graduate on time, regardless of my accident, which I was truly happy to later learn. It took me years to understand her reaction to my situation. But in the end, I understood that she was frightened and alone. I was the one that was physically hurt. She was the one that was emotionally terrified. She did the best she could do, and she had nothing else let to give.

While my mother was cleaning out our apartment, she went through all my things. My roommate and I had made a secret pact that we would hide anything questionable from each other's parents if at any time one of us needed to protect the other. In my case, I had acquired a diaphragm from the college infirmary. I had never used it, as I was still mortified over my "Peter Experiment." I specifically ask my roomie to dispose of it if ever my mother is nosing around in my things. She didn't. She was too busy trying to get through this unfortunate uproar to her own life and find a place to stay. My diaphragm was the least of her worries. It never crossed her mind.

My mother found it. In one of the most horrible moments of my life, I can still see and hear my mother coming into the hospital room and shaking me awake. I was so sick. She bent over me with crazy eyes showing me what she had found. She screamed at me and started to interrogate me about my sexual activity. That was the first of several times that I would ask God if I could please die. I was totally locked in this bed and would be going home to this unstable woman who would emotionally punish me every day. Why couldn't I just have died in the accident?

Two days after my accident, word was out that I was in bad shape. So, who would show up at my hospital bed but that same football guy who had hurt me over and over again? He even dropped out of grad school for that semester in order to sit by my side. He came every day. He sat by my bed. He never missed a day. Nothing could have been better than what he was doing for me. This totally changed everything for me. I had been so in love with him and when he heard what happened to me, he rushed to my side. It was the love commitment that I had dreamed of all through school. For weeks, he supported me. He knew the nurses. They all loved him. They all congratulated me for having such a knight in shining amour. Even though I was broken and in so much pain, I had never been that emotionally excited.

Three weeks into my recovery, the doctor came in to tell me that he had done all he could do with my left ankle. I'd had three surgeries on it since the accident, but he explained that the damage to the ankle was beyond repair. He literally looked at me and suggested that I consider an amputation at the ankle and a prosthetic. My loyal football boyfriend was sitting beside me. My parents were staring. There was silence. I quietly cried. I just wanted to be alone. Everyone left for the night. I stared at the ceiling and once again wondered what the point of my life was.

The next morning, my knight returned as usual. He brought flowers and the newspaper. We had a lovely morning discussing the news and the weather. Neither of us talked about the previous night. He made me laugh as we shared the hospital breakfast. Only after breakfast, when the nurses were done with my meds, did he look straight at me and told me that he loved me, however, he could *not* spend his life with a disabled partner. He apologized and explained that he just wanted to be honest with me. It was like he hit me square in the head with a brick. He kissed me on the cheek and left the hospital. Just like that! Done... again. That day lasted years as I cried myself to sleep. But, after all of these years later, I must admit that it would have been very difficult for a twenty-four-year-old guy to take on that responsibility. I didn't blame him. (Ironically, I eventually had my ankle fused and it has never given me a problem. To this day, you would never know I have a disability. Perhaps he made the wrong call, or perhaps he just needed a ticket out.)

Now all I had to look forward was being released to my parent's care to live in my tiny childhood bedroom again until I figured out what to do next. I knew that my mother would be emotionally unstable, and my life would be worse than a nightmare.

Note to self: As absolutely dark as my future appeared, there must have been a purpose for my life, or this accident would've ended very differently. Hold on to that thought.

Chapter Five

PEOPLE GET MARRIED FOR MANY REASONS. WE'D LIKE TO BE-lieve we all fall in love and marry our soulmate. 'Tis not the case. If we are truly honest, we marry for many reasons. In my case, it is vividly clear to me now, that my first marriage was my ticket out of a dismal situation.

A close friend of my "failed knight" heard of my accident. I didn't know him well, although we went to the same college; he was three years ahead of me. He had a great reputation for being a quiet, smart guy with the body of a Greek god. However, our paths never crossed in school. He was an athlete like my "failed knight," so they knew each other. This guy had graduated from our college and joined the USMC as an officer. It just so happened that he came home on leave from a deployment overseas not long after my accident. He'd heard of my accident. A mutual friend of ours was coming to visit me so he decided to come along. But the truth was, I believe, he didn't know many girls since he'd been away. He remem-bered that in my college years I was hot and now vulnerable and alone. Maybe I'd be an easy date. There was nothing to lose.

It was a pleasant visit. I was embarrassed by how unattractive I felt without makeup or a nice hairdo. Surprisingly, he didn't seem to notice.

Great start. My parents were thrilled because he was an officer and a gentleman with a very promising career. He kept them entertained all evening talking about his military experiences thus far. He wasn't drop dead gorgeous but handsome enough. He seemed very smart. I've always been attracted to smart men.

He continued to visit me while on leave. After several visits, he actually came to the hospital and asked the doctors if he could take me to dinner in the hospital cafeteria. He literally carried me to the cafeteria. The nurses and my parents fell in love with him. I didn't, but I was working on it. That was the evening that my mother decided he would be the perfect husband for me. Me? Well...I decided that he would be my ticket out of hell. So, I forced myself to see only his positive qualities. I overlooked anything that didn't attract me. At twenty-one years old, I had no hope of doing any better. I convinced myself that if two people are nice and compatible, love is something that will grow with time.

He left to go back to active duty, and I was released to my parent's home. I was trapped like a little child. I couldn't do anything independently, so my mother was with me all the time. She had a job as a part-time receptionist, but took a leave of absence to help me. It was awful. I was prisoner in my own house and an audience for her emotional torture. It got to be so difficult that I secretly called my grandmother and begged her to convince my mother to go back to her small office job. I begged my grandmother to have my grandfather drop her off each day to help me until I healed. Then my mother could go to work and let me heal in peace. My plan worked. My grandmother was a wonderful nurse. She did exactly what I always wished my mother would do for me. My mother never knew that I arranged it, and I had to complain about my grandmother each night so my mother would not be jealous.

During this time, my officer and gentleman wrote and called. He was attentive and pleasant. He wasn't the easiest guy to converse with over the phone because of his quiet disposition. So, I would study the newspaper daily just to have interesting things to discuss. I was healing and starting to be able to move around. I was determined to show the doctor that my ankle would heal, if not perfectly, at least enough to use. I finally was able to get up on crutches. One leg had a walking cast, and the other leg had a splint. They had surgically planted rods from my shoulders to my elbows in my broken arms so I could use the crutches. It worked!

As fate would have it, I received a letter from my university saying there would be five openings for an all-expense paid fellowship program starting in the next month. These five candidates had to have their Bachelor's of Science in Elementary Education. Through this fellowship program the candidates would earn a master's degree in Elementary Reading.The candidates would teach all day at a public elementary school and take classes in the evenings. It would take a complete year without any breaks. To my greatest surprise, the university invited me to be one of the Fellows in the program!

Within a month of that letter, I was back at the university in an apartment, waiting to begin. I had a wheelchair and a set of crutches. It was not going to be easy, but this was exactly what I needed to do. The year was a challenge on many levels, but I hung in there and graduated with a masters. I was on the crutches for that entire year and even received my diploma using crutches. In the meantime, my Marine continued to write and call. I had turned twenty-two years old during that year. He came home on leave. He went to my dad and asked permission to marry me. Then he took me out and gave me a lovely solitaire engagement ring and asked me to be his wife. He told me that we would live in many places and have interesting adventures. I knew (in my heart) that I was not in love him. But I loved the way he treated me. He would be the hero to take me away from this hell. I convinced myself that in time I would fall in love with him.

At twenty-three years old, I married. I was moved around to different states with my career Marine. At first it was exciting to see different places since I had not lived outside my radius of fifty miles from home. He was a good provider and protector, and a calm individual. Nothing rattled his feathers. He was smart and I knew that I did the right thing as far as marrying a guy with great genes. I loved that he was intelligent, as I never believed my father was smart. I loved that he was calm and didn't yell. I loved that he was making a decent income, so money was not a concern. For the first few weeks, I felt very good about my decision. I was so pleased that I had the foresight to choose this man.

But like anything in life, there is always a flip side to every situation. I know I needed a man who was calm and unfazed. He never screamed and yelled. He never argued with me. However, he was never excited either. There was no romance. Our daily talks involved making plans about the future, saving money, and discussing current events. I was not told that I was loved or appreciated. I was not told that I was beautiful. There was no playfulness. It started to become clear to me that like everything else in his military career, he was given what he needed. I was just one more thing he needed. Once I won an essay contest for a newspaper yet he dismissed it as frivolous and too emotional. He didn't see my best qualities or if he did, he didn't value them.

As he progressed through his career, I was there to do the laundry, make dinner, clean the house, and look nice at the functions. I was nothing more than one more piece of equipment he needed to become successful in his career. Very slowly, I started to emotionally wilt. I was not held or kissed. I was not stroked or embraced. We did not make love. Instead, I was awakened in the middle of the night when he needed to release. There was no foreplay. It was awful. I had traded one unhealthy lifestyle for another. This one was quiet and calm, but so lonely and sterile.

As fate would have it, the Marine Corps decided to put him through law school to become a JAG officer. Our parents were ecstatic that he was going to be an attorney. My husband was going to be an attorney! In my parents' minds, nothing could be better for me. I would be set for life. At that time, we lived in a cold northern city for three years while he attended law school. I had a difficult time finding a teaching position, so I bounced around from school to school, trying to substitute. It was difficult work, and I was inexperienced.

He took his responsibility as a law student extremely seriously. He was being paid to attend law school, so he could not fail. This determined mentality added to my lonely life. I spent days and hours by myself while he studied. I was alone more than I'd ever been in my life. Finally, I found an abandoned dog. I became very attached to that dog in order to fill my loneliness. That dog provided companionship for me. Toward the end of the second year, I asked if we could start to think about having a baby. A baby would change my life, I was sure. He said, "NO." Even though I had waited, he said it was too soon. He didn't want to be distracted in any way.

Finally at the end of the third year, I begged him to reconsider. With absolutely no enthusiasm or passion, I became pregnant. We had been married five years by then. I was convinced that finally my life would be perfect.

I had two babies in twenty-two months. Both were born in a gray, windowless Navy hospital. I had to have C-sections each time. My birth experiences were cold and callous. Like everything else, I felt ill-prepared to know what to do. I cried with fear and pain and the Navy doctor fussed at me. There was nothing memorable about their births. Their father was in attendance for both births, but he was of no emotional support to me. He simply told me that live childbirth was what every mammal does. It has been happening for thousands of years and I was no different than any other woman. I was overreacting and needed to calm down and have the baby. I was not any special medical case and the babies needed to be born. It was miserable experience.

Afterwards, we lived in a log cabin in the woods. He built it. It was his dream. I found myself slowly dying in that log cabin. It was on a dirt road, out in the country. I couldn't even use a stroller to walk the babies. I was terribly isolated and alone. I would sit on the front porch, holding a baby and listening to the birds in the forest. It could have been a peaceful, lovely place had I been in a different time of my life. But it was a recipe for disaster for a military wife with no family support and a husband who traveled. Again, my needs were not taken into consideration. I was just there to please. I was so glad to see him at the end of each day just to have a conversation with an adult. However, he was usually too tired to talk and only had time to entertain the babies before their bedtime.

I have always been good at bringing people together. So, I tried to combat my loneliness with starting a Book Club. That was helpful just to be able to be with thinking adults. Then I took it one step further and got hired to work on Friday evenings at a tiny bookshop in the small town. Friday nights were my escape, and their dad took care of the babies. I would lose myself among the books and smell the leather and printed pages. People would ask me about the books, and it felt so great to be respected as an educated person.

Eventually we were transferred to another city in the Northeast. He flew there before me and bought an old house in the town. The problem was that my husband bought this house without me seeing it. I will never forget my first impression when I walked into the house. I wanted to cry. It needed so much work. He was thrilled because he loved to do carpentry. I was devastated, knowing that any spare time that he might have, he would be repairing this old house. I cried myself to sleep once more.

Since this old house sat on a city street, at least there were people to wave to me as they passed my front porch. I would sit on the porch for hours as my toddlers played around me, just to feel like I was alive in the world. I remember befriending the walking mailman just to have a daily conversation with an adult. How pathetic that I would wait for the mail just to have someone to chat with between the feedings and the naps.

Three years into our living in this house, my life took a drastic change in direction. My husband of ten years came home with flowers one day. I was so surprised and pleased as he had never done this before. I was very touched; and I tried to feel more romantic toward him. I had put the babies to bed and came downstairs. I took a huge risk by going directly over to him and I sat on his lap. I had never done this before, but he had flowers and I thought this was a milestone in our unhappy union. He was not a man who was comfortable with outward displays of affection. But I thought I would try since he'd tried to be romantic. We had been married ten years and maybe he finally understood my needs.

He looked surprised as I sat on his lap and hugged him. Then I had the biggest shock of my life, he looked me in the eyes and point blankly said he thought we needed to get a divorce. Just like that! I was in shock.

I just stared at him. Don't get me wrong...I had fantasies of being away from this regimented life many times, but I would have never considered this as an option. It was just not in my realm of thought. Yet...I was so unhappy. But to hear he wanted a divorce, hit me like a freight train. Try to understand how it feels to experience a combination of total relief and parallelizing fear all at the same time. I had never been so emotionally confused and traumatized. My body started to shake out of control. I couldn't stop it. I will never forget the sensation. It was an uncontrollable trembling much like one would experience if freezing to death or spiking a very high fever.

Eventually I simply got up and walked across the room and sat in a chair. He went on to say that he felt we were not compatible and were not best friends. He told me we were young, and life is too long to live with someone who you don't fully love. Although I did agree with him, I would *never* have done this. I was raised Catholic! I was raised to please everyone and not consider my needs. This man was giving me an out. He said he wanted me to be happy for the rest of my life. He said he needed to be with someone who liked to do the things he liked. He said it was only fair to let me go so I no longer suffered with neck aches and back pain.

Then in the next moment he looked me square in the face and asked me where I want to move with the kids. Are you kidding? He waited for an answer. I was supposed to make a life-changing decision at that very moment. He told me to pick a city. He said he would prefer it to be on the East Coast so he would be able to visit the children with ease, since that was where the bases were located.

At thirty-three years old, I had thought I had done everything right... only to feel like someone kicked me in the chest. I couldn't breathe. I couldn't think. I was in our house of three years in the Northeast with my two preschooler's asleep upstairs, looking at my husband who promised to love me and take care of us forever. He was asking me where I wanted to move! There had to be more to this story, however I would never know the truth.

Without any research, logical thought, or experience, I blurted out "Charleston, SC." Why there? I'm embarrassed to say that I chose it *only* because it doesn't snow there. I would never have to drive on icy, snowy roads again, especially alone. I had seen beautiful photos of the historic plantations, antebellum mansions, and endless flower gardens. I figured those were enough reasons to provide happiness. That is exactly how simple my decision was. No forethought, no guidance, no help. Did I have any idea about the political views in Charleston? No. Did I have any idea about the religious beliefs in Charleston? No. Did I understand the racial bias in Charleston. No. Had I ever been to Charleston? No. Did I have any friends or relatives in Charleston? No. How absolutely ludicrous was this decision! Little did I know that living in the Deep South for me would be like living as a fish without water. But once again in my life...I had no one to ask, no guidance.

My JAG officer husband grabbed the idea of moving us to Charleston and ran with it. He could be stationed in the South easily, which would make it convenient to see the babies. Before the sun came up the next morning, he was making arrangements to move us to Charleston.

One of the most difficult things I've ever done was to call my parents. I have never done anything except try to please them, keep them happy, and make them proud and comfortable. My Catholic mother was absolutely hysterical. My German father was absolutely livid. They tried to talk me out of the decision. Then they ordered me to move back home with the kids. That was *never* an option in my mind. That would be like jumping back into hell. I tried to explain to them how emotionally ill my body had become. I tried to defend my husband for doing this in my best interest. I explained that I was seeing doctors weekly for a neck condition where I couldn't even turn sideways. I was living in such physical pain, but no one could find out the cause. My husband knew in his heart that I was slowly dying on the vine. Although I was heartbroken, frightened, confused, overwhelmed, and desperately unhappy...I still thank him to this day, in my heart, for releasing me from his hold.

The following week, he drove our three-year-old and almost five-year-old down the turnpike, where he met my dad and my younger brother halfway to Pittsburgh. Imagine my father's anger...he simply took the kids and didn't say a word. To the day he died, he'd never understand how a father could hand off two babies and drive away. And let's remember that my dad was certainly *not* the Father of the Year.

My brother was kind enough to give me his airline points to buy a plane ticket to Charleston so I could find an apartment and a teaching job. He traveled a lot and had many free miles. For ten years, I had followed this Marine officer and his career. Now I was flying alone into a new city, knocking on school doors to seek employment. The children and I had never lived in an apartment. I wasn't even sure what part of the city to search for one. I was flying to a strange city to set up a life on my own. I had few skills. I had no friends.

Because of my M Ed and my reading specialist certificate, I was immediately offered three teaching positions. I was not in a situation to be overly choosy. However, it was late October, and any seasoned teacher knows that if there is an opening in October...it's not a dream position. The teacher had probably walked out because the class was impossible to control. Sure enough, this was the case in all three positions. So, it wasn't a question of which one was the best fit...it became a matter of logistics and which principal seemed the kindest. I found a three-bedroom apartment on the first floor of a large complex close to the school I chose and signed a six-month lease. Then I accepted a fifth-grade teaching position for a class of underprivileged children living in a project. Need I say more? It was not going to be easy on any level. But I did listen to my gut, I chose the nicest of the three principals to be my new boss. Kindness matters.

Since the children were safely with my parents, I returned home and began the haunting task of breaking down the house. I had to pack all of their toys, clothes, my clothes, and some pieces of furniture to get me started. My husband rented a U-Haul and filled it to the top with things we needed. Within two days, I was following him in our minivan from New England to Charleston. We drove straight through, because that's what he does. We pulled up to the apartment building and he unloaded everything out of the van and the U-Haul. He put together the twin beds for the children and he wished me luck, gave me a hug, and left. He was driving to Washington DC to compete in the Marine Corps Marathon in the next few days. Later I would be told that he did run that marathon and was quite ill afterward. His body ached; my heart ached.

So, there I stood, alone for the first time in ten years. The emotions were epic. I felt so desperately sad, scared, and lonely. Yet for the first time in years, I was free from him. I had to work fast; I was to start my new teaching position in three days. I arranged for my mom to fly to Charleston from Pittsburgh with my two babies. I will never forget this time in my life. This was the first and last time my mom was a mother to me. This was the first time it wasn't about her. It was about me. She stayed for a few days as I began my teaching position. She loved on the kids, and she loved on me.

Finally, it was time for me to find a daycare for them. I knew no one in Charleston to take care of them. They'd been fortunate enough to have had a stay-at-home mom during their early years. But that did not make it easier on them or me to drop them at a strange place at 7am and pick them up at 4 pm five days a week. They had never been without me. It was truly awful. My daughter was born independent and did better than my son. But every morning, I literally had to peel his little body off of me and walk out of that daycare door emotionally deflated and into a classroom of total dysfunction.

Mom stayed until I got them settled in the daycare and then flew home. But every evening while she was there, she'd watch me make their dinner, do their baths, read their stories, and put them to bed. Then I'd have two or three more hours of schoolwork. One evening, she just broke down and sobbed, wondering how I was going to do this all alone. All I could say to her was, "Mom, I will be fine. I am strong and will make a life for these babies and myself. Do not worry about me. Take care of yourself and Daddy." What I didn't know was that this was to be the last time I would ever see my mom alive. My despair and pain were only going to increase tenfold.

Note to self: Never miss an opportunity to tell your Momma that you love her, even if she's far from perfect. She's the only Mom you have, and she loves you.

Chapter Six

FOR THE NEXT FEW MONTHS, I WAS LIVING ON A TREADMILL, just trying to survive. I went high speed at everything that needed to be done. It was truly a time of basic survival for the children and me, nothing more. The only fun we squeezed in was a push on the swing sets at the condominium common ground.

One evening in late December, after dark, my phone rang. It seldom rang, for I had established very few relationships at this early time. I literally jumped. I was in the tiny kitchen getting dinner for the kids. On the other end of the phone was my mom. She was in her familiar state of distress. I raised my eyebrows, but never let on that I was exhausted and irritated. It had always been my job to be there for her. I immediately tried to talk her down to calm her.

What's wrong now? I wondered. I had little to no emotional energy to spare for anyone. But as always, I pulled it together, asking her what was wrong. She cried about Dad retiring after Christmas and what that would mean for them. She was terrified for them to be together all day, every day. Too much time together was not a good thing. Yet at the same time, she complained that he'd spend all of his time golfing. I tried to explain that all couples go through a tricky transitional time when careers end. It will work out. You will fall into a new pattern. Just relax and be patient. Dad had worked for forty years, now it's time for both of you to find your new reality. But then she interrupted, saying that the doctor had found a lump on Dad's throat when he had his retirement physical. The doctor wants to do a biopsy. Again, I consoled her, saying this is a very common thing as you age. Let's not worry until we know more. They will remove it and he'll be fine, most of the time these bumps are benign.

Then all hell broke loose. The truth of why she called was now clear. She was crying, telling me that I needed to come home for Christmas. I needed to drive the babies to Pittsburgh to celebrate Dad's retirement and be with the family. By now she was really upset, literally begging me to come. Here is the difference of the way my mom was and how I've observed other moms to behave: she wanted me to come home for her. She had absolutely no thought of what I needed. I had spoiled her like a child. Her needs were always in the forefront. Just like that time I gave her and Dad money to take a trip for their anniversary instead of me going to Florida on Spring Break. Or secretly calling neighbors from college to ask them to invite her for coffee so she would not be lonely. It was always about her...way before me.

Then all of a sudden, she paused and moaned that she had such a terribly painful headache that it felt like there was an ice pick in her left eye. This did *not* help my guilty conscience from not wanting to go home. I tried to calm her down by speaking slowly and gently. I explained that I was not ready to face family and friends to explain my new reality. I slowly explained that I did not have the energy to drive twelve hours through the West Virginia mountains in the snow to get home. I reminded her of my fear of driving in the snow and ice. How could she ask me to do this alone with two preschoolers? I quietly told her to breathe and calm down, that everything would be all right in time.

At the very next moment, she did get quiet, and I felt some relief. But then I heard a noise that I will never forget. I heard a loud bang and a deep moan. Then there was total silence on the other end of the phone. I called out her name. I begged her to talk to me. Nothing. I started to get upset and my little ones could sense my emotions. They both hung on to my legs and started to cry. They didn't know why, they just knew that if I was upset, things weren't good in their lives. They were scared only because they felt my emotions; they were so dependent on me to keep them secure. After what seemed to be an eternity, I finally heard my dad pick up the phone. In the strangest voice ever, he told me that something was wrong with Mommy. She was on the floor and her forehead was bleeding.

I begged him to hang up the phone and call 911. I hung up and I actually tried to call 911 long distance. Not possible. I had to think quickly, knowing that my dad was in shock. Thankfully, I was from the generation that still memorized phone numbers, long before cell phones. I actually remembered our neighbor's phone number across the street. That certainly would not be the case today. I called that number and the neighbor lady answered. When she heard my voice, she immediately wanted to know if I was getting a divorce. Frantically, I interrupted her and begged her to call 911 and then run across the street to my parent's house. She stopped wanting to gossip about my horrible life and listened to my request. Fifteen minutes later, the ambulance pulled into my parents' driveway.

My dad was in shock and my mother's head was bleeding profusely from hitting the corner of the wall when she collapsed. She was rushed to the nearest hospital and pronounced brain dead. She had a brain aneurysm while talking to me on the phone. I did not know any of this at the time, I would only learn this later. No one called me to tell me what was going on; I was shaking with fear. I called the *one* teacher I thought was my friend in Charleston. I left her a frantic message asking her for help while I waited to know what was happening. She didn't answer her phone. I tried over and over. Then her phone didn't ring any more. There was just an endless busy tone. Obviously, she took the phone off the hook.

I found out later that she was entertaining and didn't want to be bothered. We have remained friendly over the many years; however, I have never forgotten what she did—well, didn't do. I later learned from her that her controlling husband didn't want me to be in her life for fear that I would influence her to leave him. So, with an empathetic heart, I did forgive her for ignoring me in my time of need. She needed that marriage more than she needed my friendship. Interestingly enough, they are still married to this day. I don't think she's had one happy day with that man, but she is financially very comfortable.

Late that night, I sat alone in the darkness of that tiny apartment, waiting to hear what was happening in Pittsburgh. Why hadn't anyone called me? Thank goodness the babies went to sleep without fuss. It seemed like hours, but the phone finally rang. It made me jump out of my skin. My older brother was on the phone, calling from his home in Florida. He said he was flying to Pittsburgh to check on Mom. I frantically asked him what had happened; what was the diagnosis? He simply said that she was in ICU being monitored. He told me that his wife would be driving from Florida to Charleston in the morning to get me and the kids and drive all of us to Pittsburgh. I pleaded with him to help me to understand why we were all heading to Pittsburgh. I had to teach school and hadn't accumulated any sick days. Was this truly necessary?

Mom already knew I could not come for Christmas. He was vague and almost heartless with me. He told me to be ready in the morning. The oddest part of this puzzling conversation with him was the one thing I remember the most. He and my sister-in-law asked me the best exit off of I-95 to use to get to Charleston,SC. I simply didn't know. I had only been there a short time. They both had a way of making me feel inadequate for not knowing the answer to such a simple question. Few memories in life linger longer than when someone tries to make you feel useless and stupid.

I called my new principal to explain as much as I knew. He was very kind; thank God I chose the kind one. He told me that Christmas break was only a week away and I was to go and not to worry. Unfortunately, the district would dock my pay due to lack of sick days, but he told me I mustn't worry. He would help me. That dear man has long passed. But his kindness would reside in my heart forever. He truly walked the walk.

It was a dreadfully long drive with two small children and my condescending sister-in-law. I pressed her hard to share more information with me. I knew she knew what was going on, but she wouldn't talk about it. Nothing. I decided to remain quiet and focused on my kids. I had called their father in New England to say I was on the way to Pittsburgh because my mom was in the hospital. I asked him to meet me at my parents' house to get the babies and take them to his parents' home. He readily agreed. I had no idea what I was heading into, but at least I would not have to worry about the kids. Their other grandparents loved them very much. They'd be in great hands.

It was dark, cold, and late when we pulled into my parents' driveway. No lights were on, no one was there. To his credit, the kids' dad was waiting in his car in the driveway. One of his most admirable qualities is that he can always be depended on no matter the situation. I was grateful. He quickly whisked the children away. They were elated to see him and even more elated to be going to his parents' home, whom they loved very much. They would have a wonderful time. What a relief.

We immediately headed to the local hospital where Mom was. Christmas lights were everywhere. But as we entered the hospital, everything was quiet. It was certainly not festive. My two brothers and my dad met me at the lobby door and sat me down. They scared me. They told me that what I was about to see was going to shock me and be traumatizing. I literally was shaking because no one really had prepared me. What the hell was going on? I secretly had convinced myself that she had passed out from a heart attack or high blood pressure. I knew her blood pressure was always high, and she had herself in a frenzy.

I slowly entered her room. She was lying on her back, breathing through a ventilator. I had never seen this before. Her chest was slowly and consistently rising and falling without missing a beat. She looked beautifully peaceful to me. She did not look upset or in pain. I was truly relieved. I actually remember thinking what a lovely face she had. Her skin was so soft and clear. There was not a wrinkle on her face. She actually looked radiant. I distinctly remember saying to my brothers and dad that I was relieved to see her so relaxed and peacefully resting. I still had no idea of the reality of the situation.

I held her hand and told her I was there after all. I told her we'd have a nice Christmas, and she would not have to be sad anymore. I touched her face. It didn't seem real. It was warm but it almost felt plastic. Again, my inexperience with critically ill people did not help me to understand what was right in front of me.

I looked over and saw my dad was crying. I had never in thirty-two years seen him shed a tear. Then my older brother started to cry. I was staring at them in disbelief. What the hell is happening? My mother was only sixty-one years old…she'd be fine. Finally, my younger brother looked at me and said that Momma was brain dead. She had had a brain aneurysm and she'd died instantly. There was no functioning in her brain stem. If the ventilator was not attached to her, she wouldn't be breathing. Then they said the worst thing they could have ever said to me. I will never forget these words or my heartache for the rest of my life. They said that she was so upset over my marriage separation, not moving back to Pittsburgh, and my not coming home for the holidays that she couldn't take it. That's why she died—talking to me on the phone.

I stared at all of them. I looked at her. I grabbed my mom. It couldn't possibly be true. I hugged her and sobbed on her chest. I begged her not to die. I begged her not to leave me. I begged her to help me. Please be a mom to me. I can't do any of this without you. Please, Mom, please. Then I ran from the room sobbing until I found the small chapel in the hospital. I was the only one in the chapel. I did not turn on the lights. I did not want to be found. I prayed harder than I have ever done before. I cried so hard that I could hardly catch my breath. I knelt on the hard floor, hoping that if it hurt enough, God would feel sorry for me and listen to my plea. I cried and prayed for hours it seemed. Then I lied down on the pew, totally emotionally exhausted, soaking wet with tears and sweat, and my body fell asleep. I did not want to be found. I wanted to be left alone. Just like when I was a little girl and my world was falling apart, I went to sleep to escape the pain. I wanted to die with my mom.

I have no idea how long I was in the chapel. I just know that someone very gently touched my arm and asked me if I was OK. I have no idea to this day who that was. I have never had a sister. I have never had a female to guide me or love me unconditionally. All I remember is blinking as I awoke and seeing the image of a beautiful woman standing over me smiling gently. I'd never met her before this moment. I told her that I was fine and needed to get back to find my mom, who was very sick. She very gently hugged my shoulder as I stood and adjusted my disheveled clothes and flattened my messy hair. But then as I turned to leave, she was gone. How did she leave so quickly without me being able to thank her for her kindness? Where did she go? To this day, I believe that there are angels surrounding us. I will breathe my last breath someday, knowing that on this Earth, there are angels among us. They are here for us in our darkest hours and their sole purpose is to hold us up when we cannot hold ourselves up alone.

For the next few painful days, we sat next to Mom. I know we all thought that just maybe there had been a mistake. Maybe there would be a Christmas miracle and she would open her eyes. I stayed overnight with her while the boys took care of Dad. He was an absolute wreck. I'm sure he was in utter shock at the thought of losing Mom. They had been together over thirty-five years. But the truth of the matter is, I think he was terrified. She took care of the money, the bills, the cooking, the laundry, the shopping. He didn't even know how to write a personal check, make a meal, or operate the washer and dryer. Interestingly enough, he was more worried about his clothes than most other items. You see, he was seriously colorblind and had never put an outfit together their entire marriage. Seems like such an obscure concern, but it terrified him.

One evening, I was alone with my mom and the neurologist came into the room. He asked if he could speak to me. He took my hand and explained that what had happened to my mother could be genetic. My brother had told him that our maternal grandmother died from a brain hemorrhage, as did Mom's sister. He said that it is not uncommon for this condition to be passed down through a family. Then he looked at me and said, "Especially to the daughters." He knew that I was an emotional wreck, but he asked me to be vigilant as I age in controlling my blood pressure and observing if I suffered from chronic headaches. He was gentle with his words, but he made sure I heard them loud and clear. Then, with tears in my eyes, I looked at him and told him that my family believes that I contributed to Mom's death. I had recently separated, moved far from my parents, and wasn't planning on coming home for Christmas for practical and emotional reasons. I was the one she was crying to on the phone when she died. He looked at me with the most endearing eyes and squeezed my hand. He told me that I had absolutely *nothing* to do with her death. Her brain had been carrying this aneurysm her entire life. The fact that she was overweight, had very high blood pressure, and was emotionally unstable gave way for that weakness to blow. It was like she was a walking time bomb and had no idea. It was just a matter of time. He told me I was never to entertain that thought again. In fact, the sole purpose of him pulling me aside was to explain that this condition is a very physical, genetic abnormality. No one can cause you to have an aneurysm. The fact that I was the last person she spoke to should be viewed as a beautiful gift of love and nothing else.

On Christmas Eve at 8:00 p.m., the doctors and nurses turned off Mom's machines. She died instantly...I guess she was not really alive. Once the machines stopped, she was silent. I kissed her and walked out into the dark night. There were snow flurries, and it was bitter cold. I just waited alone at the car for my dad and brothers. Finally, they came out of the hospital. No one spoke. We went back to Mom and Dad's house.

True to who she was, she had put up the Christmas tree and decorated the house weeks before Christmas day. There were a few gifts already under the tree. One had my name on it. I sat alone on the floor and opened it. It was a beautiful white porcelain statue of Jesus holding the hands of two tiny children, an older girl and a younger boy. It was the most beautiful thing I had ever seen. For the rest of that horrible night, I held onto that statue. I had no idea what to do next. I would never hear her voice again. I had absolutely nothing to look forward to and no one to hold me. Like a frightened child, all I could do was cry myself to sleep, wanting my mom.

Before the machines were disconnected, I very carefully breached the subject with my dad to please consider donating Mom's organs. She was the most giving human being I've ever known, and I believe with all of my heart she'd want to give one last time. She had beautiful blue eyes, a healthy heart, good kidneys, and a very healthy liver. She never drank. Think of how many people could be saved with her healthy organs. You would have though I punched him in the gut. He let out a roar. He screamed at me for even considering such an idea. There was no way anyone was going to cut her up as if she was at the butcher shop. There was absolutely no reasoning with him. I got quiet and simply lowered my head. My brothers scowled at me in disbelief. Although I knew she'd want this to happen, I kept my mouth shut.

That Christmas week was a flurry of unhappy activities. Dad only wanted one morning of viewing for Mom. That limited many people from coming. Then he had her body buried the very next morning. My children's father did not bring them to say goodbye to their grandmother—he decided they were too young—nor did he or his parents come. This hurt deeply because the two sets of grandparents had vacationed together on a few occasions. This was the same guy who asked my dad permission to marry me and promised to take care of me forever. This is also the guy my parents drove hours for to attend his promotion ceremony when he was promoted in the Marine Corps. Even though our marriage was dissolving, he was still part of my family. So much for promises. So much for believing in stupid romantic fairytales.

I stood alone through the whole painful process. Looking back, perhaps it was better that he didn't show. My dad was so emotionally unstable, it could have been ugly. I remember going to the horrible, dirty K-Mart near their house, hoping to find a black dress to wear. I didn't find one. I distinctly remember not feeling comfortable in what I wore. I just wanted to feel good and to have a sliver of confidence throughout this entire exhausting process. But I guess it really didn't matter after all. No one cared.

Interestingly enough, my parents had purchased plots in the cemetery. I had no idea. That did make things slightly easier. She was buried with very little fanfare or sentiment. She was just gone.

By the end of that week, on New Year's Eve, I was on a plane with my two preschoolers, heading back to our apartment in Charleston. I had no choice. I had to get back to school. I will never forget sitting in the very last row of the plane. I guess we literally got the last and cheapest seats. I was fine being that far back in the plane. I could hide in the back. I was in a deep fog. I entertained the kids the best I could. The flight attendant came back to check on us. She was kind to the kids. They were well behaved, thank God. She looked at me and ask me if I had a lovely family Christmas. I couldn't stop my eyes, they began tearing. As hard as I tried, the tears came. I simply said that I just buried my mom. She was shocked, for that is not the answer she expected to hear. She brought the babies some extra goodies to eat, a special airplane pin, and an airplane coloring book with crayons. It was evident that she was heartbroken for me but didn't know what to say or do. Yet all these years later, I remember her kind eyes. She felt my deep sorrow.

When we landed, to my surprise, my principal and his wife were there to pick us up at the airport. They had a car full of groceries and a pre-cooked meal for us. They carried everything into our apartment and got our dinner ready. Talk about angels surrounding us in our time of need.

After they left and the kids were asleep, I sipped my tea and cried. It was all surreal. What am I going to do without her? How is my dad going to survive? What kind of life am I going to have in this strange new city? So many unknowns. So much fear and uncertainty. What should I do next?

It was after 11:00 p.m. and I heard someone at the door. I dared not answer it. It wasn't a knock; it was more like a scratching sound. I waited a while. Finally, after much time went by, I quietly opened the apartment door. Maybe some sweet soul left us a Christmas present. Nope. My Christmas wreath was gone. Someone had stolen my Christmas wreath right off my door. Talk about hitting a girl when she's down.

Note to self: Sometimes having a huge cry alone in the dark is the best medicine for a broken heart. It doesn't change anything, but it exhausts you and helps you fall asleep for a temporary escape from the pain.

Chapter Seven

IT'S TRULY PATHETIC TO ADMIT, BUT I LOST THE TWO MOST CRU- cial people in my life within a six-week period. My husband and my mother were both gone from my life. I was having such a difficult time trying to process this concept. How could two people whom I relied on, communicated with, and loved the most, both be gone? I was not feeling sorry for myself. Bad things happen to good people all the time. It's just that of all the people I've ever known, I never thought for a second that I'd be the one in this unfortunate situation. How did this happen?

My mantra became "Just deal with it and move on!" Much easier said than done. In fact, I'd be lying if I didn't admit to crying and hav- ing a personal pity party every single night after I got the kids to bed. So, I made up my mind to start to see the good in the situation. Find it. You have to start out small, but there is good in each day. Just find it.

For the first three decades of my life, I lived in the Northeast. I lived in dreary, cold, rainy, snowy, cloudy climates for thirty years. Now I am waking up and the sun is shining. It's shining almost every day. It's January and there are flowers blooming. Kids are wearing shorts to school. The air is breezy and light. I distinctly remember thinking how anyone could possibly be in a bad mood living in such a beautiful climate. I'd drive to school smiling every morning. Don't get me wrong; that smile usually vanished when the first school bell rang. But no matter how poorly the kids behaved, we had outdoor recess every day. I'd get to breathe the fresh air halfway through each school day. Also, my own preschoolers were able to play for hours outside at the daycare center. How wonderful for them. That would not have been the case where we had been living.

As strange as it seems, although I was lonelier and more frightened about the future than I'd ever been, losing these two fundamental people in my life was a *huge* relief. I had been pushed and pulled between the two of them for years. I tried to please my husband with his constant future planning while trying to carry my mother emotionally. At this moment, I vacillated between missing them so much that the pain would bring me to my knees and feeling an incredible sense of freedom and peace. When I felt overwhelmed by my new reality, I'd repeat my mantra and power through my day with a smile on my face.

Note to self: There is truth to the saying,
"Stop and smell the flowers."

Chapter Eight

IRONICALLY, DURING THE TIME I MOVED TO CHARLESTON, UN-beknownst to me, there was a serial rapist on the loose. Bad timing. His name was Duncan Proctor. He would crawl through first-floor windows of apartment buildings to attack his female victims. He was accused of attacking and raping at least thirty women in the Charleston area. Yes, we had a first-floor apartment. Fear was rampant throughout the city. It was all that people could think about and discuss. I guess I had so much on my mind that I tried not to dwell on this horrible predator. But I was very cautious, and we were locked down early each evening. There was no way he could get into our apartment.

The only good thing that came out of this frightening time was the children's father got wind of this news. By this time, we had been in our apartment for half of the six-month lease. He called me one evening and offered me his GI Bill (zero-down-payment loan) to look for a safer home for the three of us. I guess that news frightened him enough that he was going to make sure we were in a safer location. Once again, I re-member thinking, *always look for the good even if it comes out of the bad.* Without much trouble, I found a townhome in a lovely, quiet neigh-borhood that had great schools. Living in the South, I quickly learned that not all schools are equal. Don't kid yourself. But this neighborhood had winning schools.

I had to break our apartment lease and pay a penalty. Small price to pay for happiness. We were able to move into the townhome within the next month. The kids each had their own precious bedroom, I had a large master bedroom, there was a playroom, a loft, and a great kitchen, a dining room, and a spacious living room. It was perfect! Not to mention that I got it for a great price. I felt so blessed. Also, it was on a quiet cul-de-sac, so I did not have to worry about a busy street with small children. The best part of this neighborhood was that it had a private neighborhood pool right across the street from our townhome. As I look back on those days, the majority of our spare time was spent at the pool. It was truly the best babysitter I could have ever wanted. I will always remember that this townhouse was the very beginning of our new life in this town. The three of us finally belonged somewhere safe to call our own. Fortunately, shortly thereafter, horrible Duncan Proctor was arrested and sent to jail for life. I could sleep at night in peace.

Note to self: Keep your guard up as a single woman with two small children; you are all they have.

Chapter Nine

TO OBTAIN A DIVORCE IN SOUTH CAROLINA, YOU ARE RE-
quired to wait an entire year once you have a legal separation document.
If you spend one night with your spouse during that year, you must
start the process over. What an old fashioned and heartless law. It is an
eternity, not unlike being in limbo, to have to wait for an entire year or
more of your life. Technically you are still married, so dating is not appropriate. But to be in my early thirties and alone with two small kids, it
was a terribly lonely time. I had no way of meeting friends except other
teachers at school. But our days were so demanding, there was very little
time to mingle and establish friendships.

Therefore, I thought the best idea was to get involved in a church.
Being so opposed to Catholicism, yet not familiar with the Protestant
world, I decided my best option was to join an Episcopal church.
Their rituals are very similar to the Catholic traditions, so this might
be the perfect transition. I decided that we would attend the beautiful Episcopal church in downtown Charleston. It was gorgeous and
the people looked inviting and classy. It sat in the center of Charleston,
which was full of history and beauty. Therefore, it would be a great
reason to go to the historic part of Charleston once a week, which I

thoroughly enjoyed. So, for several weeks, the three of us attended the Sunday service. The kids loved the playroom, while I savored every moment of the service. It was a special time of deep reflection for me. I seldom could get through a service without tears rolling down my face. Every song was beautiful, and I was emotionally raw.

I noticed that after the services, everyone would gather in the gorgeous courtyard to chat. Families were together greeting neighbors and friends. Interestingly enough, it took me a few weeks to observe that although the kids and I hung around, no one ever approached us. I'd let the kids climb on the playground toys for a while and then quietly we'd head home.

Not to be defeated, I decided to join a study group at the church to meet others. After teaching all day, I would drag the kids to the church once a week for my class. It was exhausting for all three of us, but I knew I had to try to meet other adults. Three sessions into these classes, I was approached by the minister afterward. He asked me where my husband was. I explained my situation. I thought that finally someone cared enough to ask and show empathy. Finally, someone is going to welcome me into a group.

I could not be more wrong. The minister sat down with me and scolded me for not trying harder to keep my marriage together. He said we were joined in union under God, and it was my duty as a wife and mother to keep the marriage healthy. He reprimanded me for moving so far away with the kids. He said they need their father far more than I needed to be away from him. He said that in this church, the sacrament of matrimony is highly regarded. He told me that if I wasn't willing to work on my marriage, then this church was not a good fit for me.

Just try to imagine my reaction to his words. I was in shock. I just stared at him. Then I stood up and with as much dignity as I could muster, I walked away.

It was very clear to me that this congregation was comprised of generations of people who had prayed there for hundreds of years. Most of them were 'blue bloods' who lived in the expensive, historic district of downtown Charleston. Obviously, these families had money, status, a family name, and a strong Southern reputation. These were the qualities that exemplified this congregation, none of which I had. How foolish I had been to think I would be welcomed in such a place. I quietly walked away with my head down, gathered the babies from the nursery, and drove home. I never stepped foot in that church again.

Note to self: Not all religious institutions care about those lost sheep who look differently than their sheep.

Chapter Ten

THE YEAR PASSED SLOWLY. AT ONE POINT, I RECEIVED A LETTER from my ex-husband, asking my opinion about the two of us reuniting. It was written as an attorney would write it. He had the audacity to admit his lack of love and affection for me but noted that it would be a prudent financial decision to live together and raise the children. He said it was costing him a lot to travel back and forth as well as pay the child support. He said we would accumulate more money for the future, and it would be better for the children if we reunited. He even signed the letter with his three initials. I read it in disbelief.

He never mentioned anything about my feelings or my needs. Although he was correct that we would be better off financially, how could I spend another twenty years in a loveless marriage? I didn't believe it would be better for the children. We would be raising them as he was raised. His parents lived in a pragmatic union with nothing based on love or affection. That is what he learned, what he knew and practiced. But not I; there's so much more to life. This heartless letter only motivated me to sign the divorce decree faster than I had planned.

Again, he only cared about planning for the future with no thought of the emotional consequences in the least.

How I regretted agreeing to marry him at this moment. Why hadn't I listened to my gut way back then?

*Note to self: Don't compromise your soul
for practical or financial reasons.*

Chapter Eleven

WE HAD BEEN LIVING IN CHARLESTON FOR ALMOST TWO years. This second year, I was fortunate to be asked to work in a different school. It was still a school full of at-risk, lower socioeconomic students, but I was hired to create an innovative program. I did not have my own classroom. I simply provided a unique and entertaining curriculum used to enrich the students in the hopes of elevating their learning. A dream job for me. My new principal was a mover and shaker and wanted to do all sorts of nontraditional programs to put this school on the map. I loved her energy.

Work and home life had fallen nicely into place. My daughter was now in the public-school excelling, and in a year my son would join her. I was able to get her into a creative arts magnet school that was highly regarded. Because I got her into the school, my son would be guaranteed a spot. There was only one thing that was missing in my life: a social life. I was desperately missing having adult conversation and male attention. I was surrounded by women in every aspect of my life. Sometimes it's just nice to be around men. They think differently than women and I have found our conversations far more engaging and interesting than what women usually discuss. Unfortunately, things were rather quiet in my life. Pathetically, I actually enjoyed taking my son to the orthopedist when he broke his arm because the doctor engaged in interesting conversation with me. He took the time to talk to me. Then pathetically I looked forward to taking the dog to the veterinarian, because the vet loved to chat. Both of these men were married. This was not flirting. They were simply paying attention to someone who was a customer. I truly appreciated that they took the time to talk to me, for they had no idea how lonely I was. I wonder how many single people feel just like I did.

Note to self: Never miss an opportunity to chat with someone who needs a little of your attention. You have no idea what people are carrying in their hearts.

Chapter Twelve

THEN ONE DAY, IT HAPPENED. I WAS INTRODUCED TO A MAN by a sweet older neighbor lady. She was such a kind old soul; how could her judgement of a person be wrong? She said this gentleman had done carpentry work for her and was talented as well as very good looking. Apparently, he had moved to the Charleston area from Boston in 1989 after the dreadful Hurricane Hugo destroyed the Low Country. Many contractors landed in the area because there was such a need for repair work. Not to appear snobby, but I was not used to dating blue-collar men. Actually, I wasn't used to dating anyone at this point. But if I had, I would have liked to date educated men. I really was attracted to intellect. My dating history was always spent with professional men. I was a bit apprehensive. As an English teacher, I was terrified to find out that he ended his sentences with prepositions or used double negatives. I know that is so grammatically snobby of me. I took a few days to think it over, but then I agreed to meet him. You know the old saying, "Beggars can't be choosers." So why not?

It was true; he was very handsome and exceedingly attentive to me. He spoke the Queen's English too. More importantly, when I spoke, he looked me in the eyes and truly listened. After the initial meeting, each time he came to visit, he brought flowers. He was truly sweet to my children. He had never been married and had no kids of his own. A perfect dating situation for a single woman with two young children. I did see his carpentry work at the neighbor's townhome and was truly impressed. In fact, as he visited our townhome more and more, he'd mention areas that needed to be repaired or renovated. He asked me if he could help me with the house.

What did I do? I invited this man into our life, into our little world. He stepped right in and remodeled the playroom for the children. How clever of him. Nothing will win a woman over faster than being kind to her babies. Then he put a large window in an exterior wall to give us more sunlight. It totally lightened the house. His improvements continued weekly. He even volunteered to be the coach of my son's soccer team. He went to every practice and every game to help these little boys learn how to play the game. When the children had doctor's appointments on a school day or became ill at school, he was always able to gather them, so I didn't have to miss school. It was a win-win situation. I felt like I'd won the lottery.

So, what did I do next? I married him. I fuckin' married him. I completely dismissed every red flag that I had seen concerning him, and I had seen a few. At the time, the situation seemed perfect in my eyes. I felt like it was an answer to my prayers. I was lonely, the kids needed a man in their daily lives, and he would be able to help pay for the daily expenses. He was handsome, charming, and crazy about me. The best part was that he was very romantic. For ten years, I was in a marriage that was totally void of romance. Now I thought I died and went to heaven. Every day was a dream come true. He planned romantic overnights when the kids were with their dad. He'd take me to beautiful candlelit bistros in town that I never knew existed. It was perfect!

Shortly after our elopement, he mentioned that he'd like to get a nursing degree. He was very good with his hands, was extremely talented at detail work, and knew that he could always get work as a nurse. That work would be much steadier than waiting for carpentry jobs. Plus, he promised to continue his carpentry work while he went to college. It sounded like a good plan. He'd still be contributing to our household. So, for the next five years, he went to nursing school and worked. By the end of the fifth year, he had a master's degree in nursing. I had helped pay for his entire training. We scrimped for five years, not taking any vacations or doing anything extravagant in order to pay his tuition. But we both believed it would pay off in the end. The day of his graduation, we all went to the commencement. It was a big celebration, and I was very proud of my husband. Now that I look back on it, I find it ironic that Bill Cosby was the commencement speaker. That should have been a clue right then and there that there were secrets to unfold. Not everything is as it appears to be in life. Remember how we all loved Bill Cosby? Little did I know what lie ahead.

Note to self: If something seems too good to be true...run!

Chapter Thirteen

HE IMMEDIATELY GOT A NURSING POSITION AT THE MAIN HOS-
pital downtown. Life was going well. In fact, shortly thereafter, we moved
into a suburban house with a lovely yard in a great neighborhood for kids.
It was the kind of place where they could go outside to play, and I did not
have to worry. All the moms kept an eye on all the children.

One summer day when the kids were outside playing and he was
at work, I received a phone call. There was a woman on the phone, and
she called me by name. Then she continued and asked if I was married
to a nurse at the hospital. I told her I was. She proceeded to tell me that
she is a mother of a seventeen-year-old daughter who is currently in the
hospital. She informed me that my husband was one of her daughter's
nurses. She paused and emphasized to me in very strong language that I
needed to have a talk with him before he lost his job. What was she saying? I was totally confused. She continued saying that my husband has
been flirting with her daughter when she was alone. He brought her ice
cream and told her how beautiful she was. He even offered to massage
her if she'd like it. I was shaking. This couldn't be true!

I pleaded with this mother, asking her not to report anything to the
hospital administrators. I would immediately call my husband to get to

the bottom of this accusation. I told her we had two small kids, and I am a teacher. We would be in financial trouble if he lost his job. I tried to convince her that this must be a huge misunderstanding. My husband was very kind and gentle. Perhaps her daughter misunderstood his intentions. Not that I was blaming her teenager, but I do understand that sometimes starry-eyed teenage girls only see and feel what they want. Luckily, she agreed to keep this quiet as long as it was addressed immediately. Thankfully she had a heart, for she certainly did not owe me anything. She could've ruined our life as we knew it by reporting this immediately. I thanked her profusely and promised that I'd get to the bottom of this situation.

I instantly called him at the hospital. I was very upset. I told him to come home now, not at the end of his shift. I told him that we have a huge problem, but I did not tell him what was happening. He rushed home. I was crying when he got home. The kids were still outside. I looked at him in disbelief. Then I tried to tell him about the phone call as calmly as I could possibly speak. He listened in shock. Then he said he could explain. He went on to say that he thought the girl was at least twenty-one years old. (As if that matters.) She was very mature and too sophisticated to only be a teenager. He explained that he did some simple flirting with her just to have a little fun. He said it was harmless.

I asked him, how can flirting with patients be harmless no matter their age? I told him that I was devastated that not only did he flirt with a *child*, but he also cheated on this marriage by flirting with another woman. Then I asked him if he did, in fact, offer to massage her? He denied ever offering her a massage. He said he just helped her get more comfortable by adjusting her pillows and blankets. He said he was simply having some fun with an attractive patient to make his day pass at a faster pace. He said she flirted back and enjoyed his attention. He said she tempted him.

Are you kidding? *This child was seventeen!* This was not only un-ethical, but it was also illegal. He'd better pray that the mother found it in her heart not to go to the administration about his behavior. I explained that she was going to report this, and I pleaded with her, for the sake of our family, not to react until I could understand what was happening. Then I told him that this could *never* happen again. It was wrong on several levels. More than any of the hundreds of reasons why it was wrong, he had broken my spirit and trust in our marriage.

With all the right words, a very sympathetic face, loving hugs, and teary eyes, he apologized. He promised to change units and never go near that patient again. This was of little comfort to me, but at least we dodged this bullet. Little did I know that this was only the beginning of a barrage of bullets yet to come my way.

Note to self: Listen to your gut and do what you need to do and stop worrying about what others will think.

Chapter Fourteen

SIX MONTHS LATER, I WAS AT A HOLIDAY HOSPITAL FUNCTION with him. I excused myself to visit the ladies' room. I had noticed that another nurse had been staring at me during the evening. I shrugged it off as if she admired the dress I was wearing. To my surprise, she followed me into the bathroom. As I was reapplying my lipstick, she turned to me. She looked heavy-hearted and anxious. Then out of the clear blue sky, she apologized to me. I was blindsided as I looked at her, not understanding. Apologize for what? I didn't even know her name. I had never seen her before this evening.

She explained that she was feeling uncomfortable about meeting me. She said that my husband told her that I'd be fine with meeting her because the two of us had an open marriage. He told her that I would find it exciting. He promised her that I knew the two of them had been having a weekly affair for the last six months. He explained that it was my idea to have an open relationship. I started to shake and stared at this woman. What was she saying? What the hell was happening?

I ran out of the bathroom and ran into the street. I waved down the first taxi I saw. OMG. This can't be happening. What am I going to do? I need to get out of this marriage. There was danger lurking with this man. How could he deceive me like this and then tell lies about me to cover his outrageous actions? But the thought of another failed marriage—I can't leave another man. What would people say if I divorced again? What would they think? What am I going to do now? Then another horrid thought flashed into my head: what germs was he carrying? How many women had he been with since we'd been married? I swore I would never be intimate with him again. That was over. But I didn't know what to do about the marriage. I just couldn't imagine having two failed marriages.

Of course, he was pitifully sorry for his indiscretions. He begged for my understanding and forgiveness. He tried very hard to make things right again. In fact, he went so far as to surprise me with a beautiful coach trip around the UK because he knew of my love of anything English. I safely kept him at arm's length. There was no believing him anymore. I was just trying to buy time until I knew what to do next.

I decided to accept the trip. We went together, and it was a perfect trip around England. It was like a storybook tour of small villages, ancient pubs, high teas, gracious people—he even made arrangements with the children's father to keep the kids, so I did not have to worry about the children the whole time. He had it all planned perfectly. Maybe he was truly remorseful after all. But I was still so deeply wounded by his behavior. I did not welcome him back with a sweet smile and a loving hug. I just focused on the vacation of a lifetime for me and tried to put the nightmares of the last year out of my mind.

To save face, I decided that this marriage *had* to be successful. I couldn't bear the idea of having a second failed marriage. So once again, we all got back into our day-to-day lives. After the England trip, we came home and had a huge heart-to-heart talk about what needed to happen to keep this marriage alive and healthy. He was living up to his word that he would be a loyal husband and a good stepfather. He was truly trying.

Then one Saturday evening several months later, he took me to a party. He told me it was with colleagues from the hospital. We went to a lovely home, and I was introduced to the others. They were friendly and warm. They were all health care professionals. He proudly introduced me and seemed to be enjoying showing off his pretty wife. I was flattered but was still cautious. It was going to take me a while to trust him after what he had done. I thought it was a bit odd how he glided me around the room, showing me off to his friends. Then he started giving me wine glass after wine glass. I was not a drinker while I was raising my children, so after two glasses I was feeling giddy and tipsy.

That's when I realized what kind of a party this was...these people were all swingers! Two by two, they were disappearing from the main room into the various bedrooms in the house. I was in shock. That's why he was prancing me around like cattle at the livestock auction. I had to get away from there. When no one was looking, I grabbed my purse and slipped out the side door. I knew I couldn't drive. I started running and running until there was no way he'd be able to find me. (Well, if he even cared to try.) Finally, out of breath, I started walking for what seemed like miles in the dark. I saw a police car at a gas station. I walked up to his window and humbly asked him to please help me get home. He was concerned that I was hurt. I assured him I was not physically hurt, I just had too much to drink. Luckily, he asked me no further questions and very kindly drove me home. I believe to this day that he could see through my story but was considerate enough just to make sure I got home safely. I will always be grateful to that policeman.

What was I to do next? My ego could not dare let me get another divorce. I was so frightened. Look what I'd gotten myself into with this man. What could I do? Who could I talk to? No one. I suffered silently for quite a bit longer. But then I think God/the universe said *that's enough!* The universe has a way of making things happen when we are too frightened, confused, exhausted, or just plain stupid to know what to do. Never believe for a moment that there is not a greater force caring for your happiness. There is. Just trust.

A month later, I was at school one evening for a mandatory PTA meeting. My children stayed at home playing in their rooms until I got home. My husband was home too. Apparently, the kids wanted to make popcorn for a snack, so they went into the office to ask permission to make microwave popcorn. He was using the computer. The two children were dumbfounded as they noticed what was on the computer screen. Then there was a very unpleasant scene.

My daughter frantically called me in the middle of the PTA meeting. She was hysterically crying and said she walked in on him using our computer and saw naked girls on the screen. When the two kids fussed at him about what he was doing, he screamed at them and spanked them hard, telling them to mind their own business. He told them that they were nothing but two spoiled brats.

That was it. I drove as fast as I could to get home. I told him to leave. I told him if he did not leave, I would call the police. He wouldn't leave. He said his name was on the title and this was primarily his house. I had not known that he removed my name from the title. I had been too trusting. He told me if I didn't like the situation, then I needed to leave. Up to this point, he had emotionally hurt me several times, but he had never hurt my children. A mother will do *anything* to protect her children, no matter the sacrifice. I packed three bags and we left. We got in the car and drove away. I had nowhere to go. I had no one I trusted enough to call. I was so terribly embarrassed I didn't want anyone to know. I found an inexpensive hotel for the night. The next day, I took the kids to school, and I called in sick. I found a small condo not too far from our house and rented it for a month. At least we'd be safe while I figured out what to do next. I left him a message that I was coming by the next day while he was at work with a truck to get the children's clothes, toys, beds, etc. He agreed to it. I was relieved that he would not be there. I had to work fast. I hired two men to help me take as much furniture, kitchen supplies, bedding, linens, clothes, recreational items, etc. as I could fit into that truck. We filled it to the brim. I did one more walkthrough, knowing that when he came home, I'd never have a second opportunity. When he got home, he was livid. He said he felt like he had been robbed. That's when I realized what a narcissistic selfish man he was. He only cared about himself and his possessions. He immediately changed all the locks, and I was never able to set foot in that house again. Whatever I had not grabbed was disposed of or destroyed. The only thing I truly missed was my box of twenty years' worth of diaries. I had kept a diary since the day I learned to write. He burned them all.

He stayed in the house alone until he remarried. We weren't even divorced, and he remarried a bizarre woman whom he met at a swinger's party. I guess they were married, that's what he told others. Turns out that he had to give me a payout when finally, our marriage was dissolved. It was not as much as it should have been. But it was enough for a down payment on a small house for my kids and me. Remembering that I had paid for the majority of his five-year college education just cut me to the core, that now, this was all I had to show for it. However, as fate would have it, his wild lifestyle led him to having to foreclose on the house. He lost it in the end. He lost everything in the end. Karma is a bitch.

I later heard that he became sick with an autoimmune kidney disorder. The hospital had to let him go because he was missing too much work. He spent all his days in his new, lowly apartment and had a dialysis machine set up inside. He hooked himself up several times a week while he would connect with women online to visit him. From what I was told, there were women coming and going. To my horror, I was told that he even invited a teenage runaway to live there at no cost, as long as she satisfied his sexual needs when he was healthy enough to participate. How absolutely disgusting.

Eventually, I was told about a year later that he was found dead in his apartment. It turned out that the FBI had been watching him for several years. He had been involved in a child pornography ring and solicited children for sexual acts. He had been arrested and was looking at ten counts for ten years each. He would be spending the next one hundred years in prison. The coward probably took the easy way out. He probably killed himself instead of showing any remorse or retribution for his evil ways. Although, that has never been confirmed, I'm sure that was the case.

The horrible night years earlier, when the kids and I left that house and had to find a place to stay, was the very last time his name was *ever* mentioned again. To this day, decades later, my grown kids have never, ever murmured his diabolical name. In their minds, he never existed. I think that they want to believe that it had been nothing but a bad nightmare that never really happened. I will go to my grave feeling horrible that I invited him into their lives. I know they were angry with me during those turbulent teenage years probably because of this horrendous time, and I deserved it. But, in time, I hoped they would understand that if they suffered from that decision, I suffered tenfold. I hoped, instead, that they would be stronger adults because of this adversity and know that I thought I was doing something to make our lives easier. My intentions have always been in their best interest and nothing more, for I've always based my life on my love for these two precious people.

Note to self: In time, my kids will know that no one has ever been more important to me than they are, but it might take time.

Chapter Fifteen

SCHOOL BECAME MY SALVATION. I POURED MY CREATIVE ENER-gies into developing one of the most innovative curriculums around. For whatever reason, I focused my entire classroom around outer space. I had stars hanging, I had big boxes made into spaceships, I created tents that looked like a moon orbiter. The kids could crawl into these very cool places to read. I was well aware that if I wrote grants, I would be awarded money easily. Every company wanting to help teachers absolutely *love* to say they poured moneys into the underprivileged schools. It's always great PR for them. I definitely took advantage of this piece of knowledge. I wrote many grants and received lots of funding.

I established a complete space book library. I researched all the children's books and found every fictional and nonfiction book about space, the universe, stars, planets, galaxies, moons, and best of all, aliens. All of my reading, writing, and English lessons were geared toward out-er space in some fashion. The kids loved to come to my room. I was called an "Extension Teacher" because I extended the learning of the students outside their regular classroom. I was doing for the lower, un-derachieving students what G/T teachers do for the gifted and talented students.

By law, every child who qualifies as a gifted student is required to be given extra attention that teaches them concepts and problem solving that the regular classroom teacher may not have time to do. What I found most extraordinary was that I was now in my second underprivileged school, and to put it bluntly, not one student out of either of those schools had ever tested into the gifted and talented program. That means that each of these two schools had about five hundred kids each. So out of 1,000 Black students...not one was gifted. Really?

Obviously, there lies a huge problem with our educational system. I decided since I couldn't fix it alone, I would at least contribute to raising the bar. I decided that I would teach my students like we teach the G/T students. My expectations were high, but amazingly enough, the students rose to the challenge. In fact, local publications got wind of my techniques and began to run stories. Believe it or not, one thing led to another, and the next thing I knew I was being flown to the NASA headquarters in Washington, DC. I met with scientists who had been wanting to involve elementary students in the space program. Let me be truly transparent: they wanted to reach the Black community to promote the fact that all American children needed to be involved in STEM education. Not to sound cynical, I understood their bottom line. At this point, I wasn't interested in their underlying motivation; I was just pleased that my students had been noticed.

Shortly thereafter, a space shuttle was preparing for a launch. NASA specialists flew to Charleston to set up a communications station. My students were going to talk to the astronauts while in space! Think of the contrast between where these children lived, what little they had, with very limited experiences, lack of proper English, or social manners. Now these kids were going to speak directly to the astronauts while they were in the space shuttle. I certainly had my work cut out for me to get them ready. Being that I had a very assertive principal, she ran with this plan. She was beyond excited. Before I knew it, I received a call from *National Geographic Magazine.* They asked me permission to send a writer and a photographer to my classroom to cover this story. This project was spreading like wildfire. Sure enough, the kids did speak to the astronauts and their story was published in *National Geographic.* It all came together. It was truly remarkable.

Not long after this incredible experience, I heard from the director of the *USA Today* Newspaper Education Department. Apparently, this newspaper was being used in middle and high schools as supplementary reading materials for their journalism, history, and English classes. The director asked me if I would like to be their Southeastern Teacher Representative for their newspaper. She explained that they have a master teacher on board for all geographical areas of the United States. She said they saw our National Geographic/NASA project and felt I would be the perfect teacher to be on their team. For the second time in six months, I was flown to Washington, DC. It was incredible. I met this elite cadre of master teachers from all around the country. We worked as advisors to discuss and suggest how the newspaper would be used most effectively in the classroom. All of us were full-time teachers and this invitation was simply one more opportunity to expand our careers. We were treated like royalty. We would meet every quarter, four times a year, in Washington, DC.

In the meantime, I was now in my late thirties/early forties—pretty much in my prime. I was excited, enthusiastic, bright, innovative, and attractive. My teaching career was soaring. Therefore, I was elected Teacher of the Year for my school. That's a true compliment when your own colleagues vote for you as the best. The only issue with representing your school is that you were expected to take it to a higher level.

I was given a twenty-page application to complete. It was extremely detailed and time-consuming. The next step would be for the district to choose ten finalists. Charleston had over 120 schools over a ninety-mile-wide area. Therefore, the chances of being one of those ten were slight. However, I suppose my latest achievements helped me to be noticed. I was not only one of the ten, but I went on to be one of the top three Teachers of the Year for the entire county. It was truly the best thrill of my life.

When you are the top teacher for such a large county, there are some exciting perks. You are given time away from your classroom, to travel around the county in order to help struggling teachers. Each time you do this, you visit different classrooms, giving support to teachers who are in need of another set of eyes and ears. It is an incredible opportunity to help others and also to see what other teachers are doing. This experience helped me be a better teacher. This opportunity was extremely valuable to my future success as an educator.

Note to self: The best way to learn is to teach others.

Chapter Sixteen

I HAVE SHARED THIS PERSONAL SUCCESS NOT FOR THE PUR-
pose of self-elevation, but to prepare you for what is to occur because of
this sequence of events. All of these extraordinary steps that brought me
to this point, placed me in a position to make a life-changing decision.
Why this was my fate, I'm still pondering. But it happened. Nothing in
my life, as I had known it up to this point, would ever be the same again.
Unfortunately, we don't get any "do-overs" in life. Once you make a
major decision, it's yours forever. I made a huge decision.

In the meantime, let me mention that my dad had lived seventeen
years after losing my mom. He lived until he was seventy-nine, which
I consider young. To my brothers' credit, they took the role of getting
dad situated and functioning after mom died. My older brother moved
him to Florida near his home. Then the two brothers cleared out his
house, sold it, and helped him find a townhome in the same general
area. He would summer in Pittsburgh and winter in Florida. I cannot
take a lot of credit for getting him back on his feet except for my positive
phone calls and giving him emotional support. Both brothers and their
wives tried their best but drove him crazy at times. He was not a perfect
grandfather. He really wasn't interested in being one. They wanted him

to be someone he was not. I'm not sure he ever wanted to be a father, let alone a grandfather. My brothers were extremely critical of his lack of paternal involvement. I understood my dad and tried to reason with the boys. Just let him be.

Dad met a lovely widow within the first year of Mom's death. She would become a devoted partner for the rest of his years. He shared many sweet moments with her. I was very happy for him. I was actually, quite relieved that he found happiness; however, my brothers never really embraced her, they tolerated her. Dad and his lady had separate homes in Pittsburgh but wintered together in Florida. It was a peaceful existence and far happier than his life had been with my mom. So, I was simply supportive of his pleasant life and had no expectations. I never threw it back in his face, that he didn't speak to me for months when I was in my twenties and visited a man alone. Now he was living with his lady friend half the year without being married. Things had certainly changed. I forgave him for his wrath when I visited that boyfriend, but I never forgot. Talk about double standards.

I would only see him twice a year now, when he was driving past Charleston to and from to Florida. They'd visit for a few days. If anyone could have felt slighted, I was the one that could've used a father figure, being a single mother. But I understood. I have always understood who he was. It would do no good to punish him for not being what I wished he was.

Probably the most notable gesture I did to help Dad during his transition was to sew buttons on the inside of the top of his socks. Crazy, but I thought it was brilliant. Because he was totally colorblind, he could not tell a black, brown, or navy sock from each other. To him, they were all the same color. So, I bought him packages of new trouser socks. I bought dozens of different sizes and shapes of buttons. I sewed matching buttons on each pair. Then, all he had to do was match the buttons and he knew the socks would match. Black socks had round buttons, brown socks had square buttons, and blue socks had crazy shaped buttons.

This was a very successful system until one evening. He and his lady were at a formal dinner party. He was sitting cross-legged, which pushed his trouser leg to rise. He had not noticed that he was wearing his black dress socks inside out on this particular evening. A guest at the dinner saw his button on his sock. It became the center of a conversation on why he had buttons on his socks. Much laughter and joking filled the evening over my dad's socks. Unfortunately, he was a man of terrific pride and instead of laughing it off, was utterly humiliated. My gesture of love backfired. The socks were disposed of, and he only wore black socks for the rest of his life.

~

Note to self: Even your best intentions don't always work out the way you hoped.

Chapter Seventeen

AS ONE OF THE TOP TEACHERS IN THE COUNTY, I WAS THOR-
oughly enjoying helping younger and struggling teachers. Every day
was an adventure—a challenge, but very rewarding. On just a regular
Wednesday morning, I was on my way to a school in the city. I was
driving in an area in which a single woman might not want to have
car trouble alone on the road. As I drove under a railroad trestle, I saw
several school-aged children playing in the dirt. I wondered why they
weren't in school. Why hadn't anyone noticed? Certainly, a truant officer should be called. When I reached the school, I did call the central
district office, asking if someone could check on these children. There
looked to be a half dozen young Black children, from what I could tell.

Sure enough, the children and one adult woman were brought to
the school. I was there to greet them. The woman looked exhausted,
overwhelmed, unhealthy, stressed, and frightened. The administration
asked her gently why the kids weren't in school and why they were under the bridge. With great angst, she very slowly admitted that her trailer
had burned and that she and the kids were waiting for emergency housing. Getting them to school was the least of her worries. She went on to
say that only six of these children were hers. There was a seventh child;

he was her nephew. The only reason he was with them was because his mother, her sister, was an addict and alcoholic and never took care of him. She made it clear that she did not want the child, she had too many already. He just invited himself to stay with them. She explained in no uncertain terms that she thought he was disturbed.

The authorities immediately found her and the children temporary housing at a shelter. At least they'd all have a warm shower, clean beds, and hot meals while this was being sorted. But when it came time to leave, she emphatically explained that she did not want to be responsible for the seventh child, her nephew. She claimed he was like an untamed, wild dog and she could not handle any more on her plate. She told the authorities to find her sister and make her be responsible for her wild child.

He heard every word. He just stood there. He had huge dark eyes. He didn't say a word. He was a tiny boy. Although I later learned that he was eight years old, he looked more like a five-year-old. His mother was addicted during pregnancy, and he was a product of prostitution in order for her to make money for her habit. So right from the start, he had physical limitations. His face was filthy, he was obviously malnourished, he had no socks on his feet and ripped sneakers. His hair was a ball of dirt and fuzz. His appearance was truly pathetic. My heart ached for this tiny human. Evil and wild were the last two adjectives I would have used to describe him.

Without forethought, I jumped in and said that I'd like to take him home for the night. I told the authorities that I had a nine-year-old son and an eleven-year-old daughter who would be delighted to play with him. I told them that I'd give him a nice bubble bath, share my son's clothes, feed him a healthy dinner, and that he could share my son's room for the night. My own children had tons of toys that he could use. I promised to bring him back to the school in the morning.

Although this was not usually how social services operated, I begged them to let me help this child. Surprisingly, I was granted permission to take him home for the night. In my heart, I thought this would be the perfect lesson for my own kids. When something is dropped in your lap, you temporarily put your needs and desires aside to help someone less fortunate. That's how the universe works. You've got two choices: step up or step aside. I wanted to model a very important lesson for my own children. The fact that this was occurring in America in the late 20th century was difficult to believe. He walked to my car but did not open the door. I finally concluded that he did not know how to open it. He also had no idea about the seat belt. I softly asked him if he had a car and he put his head down and said, "No, ma'am." I told him that he was in for a big treat. We were going to do a drive-through at McDonald's to get me a Diet Coke and he will get to choose an ice-cream treat. Again, he looked at me dumbfounded. I realized that he did not understand. So, I simply showed him what I meant, and he smiled at the gorgeous ice cream cone that he was handed through that small window. When I think of all I did to ensure that my two children would be as healthy as possible, during my prenatal months and then after my babies were born, I was astonished by how this child has survived eight years. Who changed his diapers? Who fed him? Who cared for him? How did this baby live? Did he ever see a doctor?

.The evening proved to be an eye-opening adventure for all. I let the three children play outside after school while I prepared dinner. I could hear my daughter being a nurturing momma toward him. I could hear my son challenging him to run and ride bikes. Shockingly, he did not know how to ride a bike. So, my sweet boy tried very hard to balance him on his bike. It wasn't successful, but they laughed together. After washing hands, dinner was served. Once again, I couldn't believe it. This little boy did not understand the concept of having dinner. He didn't know to use the utensils or sit in a chair to eat. He stood until I explained the process. He hardly touched his meal except for his chicken nuggets. He never used a utensil. No vegetable or fruit touched his lips. Our family rule was that all foods had to be at least tasted and tried. My son was not happy that I was letting this child slide. Obviously, this would be a conversation for later.

When it came to bath time, I filled my large jacuzzi with warm water and lots of bubble bath. The two boys were so excited to play in the suds. My son jumped right in and started making a white beard. I helped our little visitor get undressed. To my surprise, he was wearing no socks nor underwear and his little body was filthy. The two boys had a ball playing in the bubbles. Their little fingers were wrinkled by the time I could get them out and ready for bed. I read them a bedtime story. It was the first time anyone had read to this child. Another first. Then we said our prayers, again a foreign concept.

Right before my son fell asleep, he came to find me. He whispered in my ear that he was afraid that there was something terribly wrong with our little visitor. He shyly explained that he noticed that his penis was broken. He said he noticed it when they were getting on their PJs. What my sweet son observed was that this small boy was uncircumcised. I later learned that African American boys in the Deep South were never circumcised. One more conversation that I would have to have in the future. One more thing to explain about this strange little visitor.

I returned the child to school. He looked adorable. This particular school required simple uniforms to be worn. I had grabbed a fresh set from the school surplus room and ironed them after the children were asleep. He walked into the school looking shiny clean, with new clothes, socks, sneakers that my son outgrew, and a backpack with some school supplies. I could not hide my pleasure watching him walk through the door. The administration was there and greeted him with great enthusiasm. The principal walked him to a first-grade class. Although he was eight years old, he had never been in school. Since he was so small, no one would have guessed his age. The teacher greeted him lovingly. With relief, I went on about my day, training teachers. I had told him to go to the office at dismissal and wait there. Someone would be there to take him to where he was going to live. This made him anxious, but I reassured him that I would be there too to help him meet his new friends.

The day was busy and before I knew it, the children were being dismissed. I quickly made my way to the office. There he sat, alone on a big chair; his feet couldn't reach the floor. He came running when he saw me. We chatted about his day, and I told him I'd wait with him. An hour passed and no one came. I called the social services office but could not get anyone on the phone. The administrators entered the office after dismissal was complete. They too were confused as to what to do. Where were the authorities? What were we to do with this child? We had no phone numbers of any relatives. I was feeling perturbed because I felt like I tried very hard to do what I'd said I'd do to help this child. Why weren't the people in charge doing their job?

Two hours later, I told the administrators that I had to leave. My own two children were in the after-school program, and I had to collect them. The little boy started to cry. He was frightened and didn't want me to leave. I looked at the principal and said I'd like to take him home again until we got this sorted. He did very well with my own kids, and it would be fun for them to spend another evening together playing.

Two nights turned into four, four nights into six, until finally he had been with us for weeks. I waited patiently to hear from the authorities.

In the meantime, he was blossoming in our home. A notice was sent out to any known relatives, asking for someone to come for him. No one came.

The authorities found his biological mother on the streets. She was terribly drug-addicted and an alcoholic. Of course, she could not care for him. How she was surviving on the streets was a mystery. But she did not want help. She could hardly remember him, although she was able to tell the authorities that she had older children who might be able to help. She had no idea who the father was. The older siblings were found. The sister had three illegitimate children of her own at twenty-one years old. The older brother was twenty-two years old and newly released from jail.

By this time, a very special bond of love and family was developing between my children, our guest, and myself. I stepped back from my search to find relatives and kept living our day-to-day life. It was truly sweet. Six months went by, and this child was very much attached to me. He wanted to be carried, held, hugged, read to, and was learning quickly. His language improved, as did his manners and socialization. He was quickly becoming my best-behaved child. He was just so happy to be with us, he'd do anything to please.

I visited a female attorney. I was hoping a woman might be touched by my story more than a man. (I realize I was being sexist, but it worked.) I wanted to appeal to her nurturing side. I explained my situation and asked her if she could help me pro bono. She was astonished that this child had slipped through the cracks and not placed in the foster child system or in a home for disturbed youth. I admitted that I had laid low with the rules in hopes of simply giving him stability and a strong starting point. But it was now obvious that he was going nowhere, and I'd been seriously contemplating adopting him.

This is the place in the story where I had wished someone far wiser had intervened with my decision. Here are facts: I was living in the Deep South. I was raising two kids on my own, I was a teacher working in a Right to Work state where we made minimal salaries and had no representation. Now I was about to adopt a Black child on my own. Not to mention that he would most definitely have serious learning disabilities due to his mother's addictions. In my naive mind, I was sure that love trumped everything. If I loved this small child for the rest of his childhood and raised him like my own, he would have a fighting chance as an adult. I was so sure. Years later, I would realize that this was one of the worst decisions I would make in my life. "All you need is love" is not a true phrase, as I would soon learn.

The attorney agreed to help me. We went through the entire process of what parents must do to adopt a child. I passed with flying colors. The fact that I was single was not a negative due to my status as a master teacher. There were certified letters delivered to every relative. The letter stated that on a particular date in six weeks, we would be in court to finalize the adoption. They had six weeks to stop the process. They were welcome to show up at court that day to stop the adoption. A few days after the letters were delivered, I received a phone call from the aunt who'd left him at the school and took her six kids to the shelter. She begged me to proceed with the adoption. She said it would be the only chance that kid had to have a life. She said she felt strongly that if I did not save him, he would never live to see twenty years old. She had witnessed his deep anger and violence. She was sure he'd commit a crime and eventually be shot. Who was she referring to in this conversation? The child in my home was a gentle, loving angel. Her phone call frightened me, but I brushed it off as an irrational, unstable woman, not knowing what she was saying.

The adoption day was here. Up to this point, no one opposed the adoption. No one contacted the attorney. So, the four of stood in the court in our Sunday best clothes and waited. No one came. The judge quietly proceeded with the legal adoption, and within minutes, I had a second son. It was a joyous day for us. To be perfectly honest, my own two kids acted like they had just gotten their first puppy. They loved him but treated him much like you would a new pet. It was clear they did not view him as an equal. They loved him like a cuddly bear. Since this was his big day, he was allowed to decide where to go to celebrate. He picked a pancake house for his adoption day celebration. All he wanted were *penny-cakes,* as he called them.

Note to self: Think with your brain, not with your heart!

Chapter Eighteen

LIKE ANY NEW MARRIAGE, THE ADOPTION HONEYMOON PERI-od was pure joy. Neighbors, colleagues, and friends welcomed our new addition. I even had a picnic so friends could come to celebrate. Of course, the South is still really segregated. We happened to live in a lily-white neighborhood. My new son stuck out like a sore thumb, but neither he nor anyone else seemed to notice or mind. Everyone was glad he was there. He truly became somewhat of the mascot for all the neighborhood children. He got along with everyone, and they all fol-lowed him like the Pied Piper. He played with the younger children. He had missed so much of his younger, developing years, he was thrilled to watch childish videos and play with six-year-olds. In the meantime, his brother was in a very different place with kids his own age, so the two brothers did not play together unless there was no one else around. My daughter was lightyears ahead in maturity and didn't interact with him much either. If she was free in the evening, I would see her reading to him. He still could not read. So, he'd bring her books to read to him and they'd cuddle. It was sweet.

I decided to transfer him to the same school that my two attended. It was a wonderful magnet school in which parents placed their kids on long waiting lists when they are born, hoping to be chosen. Because his siblings went there, he was automatically accepted. The teachers embraced him immediately. He was adorable with his big dark eyes and cute grin. There were few Black students in this magnet school. Again, because he was different, he immediately attracted lots of positive attention. But as we all know, hindsight is 20/20. I probably should have let him remain in the school where he was, for this new magnet school was way out of his league.

He was tested and it was determined that he had a low IQ and therefore would be a considered a slow learner. In the public school system, that was not enough to provide him with any special services. He would just trudge through school at a lower, slower pace. With students such as him, this often led to early high school drop-out. So, I intervened and ask the teacher who tested him to do me a professional favor. She agreed and had him labeled dyslexic with signs of attention deficit disorder. With these two labels, I was able to get him help from a resource teacher. He was able to get a 504 plan and have an IEP (Individual Educational Program). I knew I would need help to get him through school. I called in this favor and was very grateful to my colleague who helped me. To be honest, I had low expectations for him. I simply wanted him to graduate from high school and stay out of jail. Sad, but true. I know I could keep him healthy and meet his basic needs. But in my heart, I entered this task of raising him with very real expectations and I knew I was going to need a lot of help.

Note to self: Be your child's advocate. Go to bat for him! No one else will care more than you about your child's educational needs.

Chapter Nineteen

HIS TEETH WERE ROTTEN AND MISSING FROM HIS LOUSY DIET and lack of dental hygiene. It's cute to have missing teeth when you're six years old, but I knew this had to be addressed sooner rather than later. My other two were seeing an orthodontist by this time. They each had braces. I spoke to this kind dentist, explaining that this child would need extensive dental work. I explained that it would be very difficult for me to finance yet another set of braces on a teacher's salary.

I will forever be grateful that he and his colleague, an oral surgeon, took this child on at no cost. His rotten teeth were removed. He was given his first set of braces at nine years old to guide his teeth. His dental treatments went on for six years with these two very generous and kind men. I never paid a dime. By the time he was in his mid-teens, he had the most beautiful straight, white teeth in the city. He was extremely proud of his smile, as was I.

During those first couple of years, I had to deal with many issues that I had never considered. He could steal better than anyone around. Every time we'd get home from a store, I'd check his pockets. I returned to at least a half dozen stores, taking him to the manager to apologize and return what he'd stolen. Finally, he realized it was not worth stealing because I'd march him right back, and that was embarrassing. Plus, he finally understood that if he needed something, he simply should ask me. It's understandable that he was such a skilled thief. I'm sure that is much of how he ate his first eight years of life.

When I think of those early developmental years, I reflect on all that I did to give my two kids everything they needed. I have wondered more times than I can count how he survived those first eight years. Diapers? Toilet training? Vaccinations? Earaches? Sickness? Clothes? Housing? Vitamins? Pediatrician check-ups? To this day, I have no understanding how this kid made it this far. I suppose the stealing didn't alarm me, I just had to redirect that bad habit.

Over these years, the father of my two kids came to take them for weekends. He was a devoted father even from a distance. He would take them to the beach, camping, and hiking. However, he never included their new brother. Every time the older kids were with their dad, it would be just him and me. At first, it was nice because I could really focus on him. But as the years went by, I'd see how he felt when his siblings would go off on big adventures and leave him home. I realized their dad had absolutely no obligation to include him. I just wish he'd had a few of those camping experiences.

School became harder with every passing grade. I spoon fed him through school. I hired a college student to tutor him; I relied heavily on his resource teacher to help him to be as successful as possible. It was a struggle. By fifth grade, he was still a nonreader. He was promoted each year, but his deficiencies became more apparent with every promotion. I am grateful that he behaved even though I have to believe he was terribly frustrated. Each award ceremony, he received an award; usually for the hardest worker, or for being a good citizen. But to be honest, perhaps he was not smart enough to even know his shortcomings.

The teenage years became turbulent in our house. My older son was not a school-prone kid. In middle school, he started to skip school. He was caught with pot. Up to age fourteen, he had lived with me and was truly the love of my life. But now, he hated school and wouldn't listen to me. He fought about doing chores, homework, friends, etc. He basically turned our home into a horrible place to live. In the meantime, my daughter was having her own self-esteem issues. School was easy for her, and she always academically excelled. However, she did not excel socially. She had a few friends, but most kids found her pushy and difficult because she was far ahead of most of her peers. She absolutely looked at me with disgust at least six times a day. I could say nothing or do nothing right. I realize this is typical of mother/daughter teen years, but I think it was more involved. I believe she was just downright angry with me about how her life was going. Our home was beginning to be a nightmare on a daily basis. For fourteen years I was the sole parent of these three kids. I thought I was doing the best job possible. But all hell was about to break lose.

In the meantime, my adopted son had many friends and fans in the neighborhood. He was so easy-going, spoke beautifully now, was extraordinarily polite. Everyone adored him. I'm thinking they were all astonished by how far he'd come. People actually stated that he spoke "like a white person," which is about as politically incorrect as it gets. But it was the truth. I would hear him saying phrases like, "No ma'am, I'm not fond of vegetables," or "Ma'am, may I use your restroom?" or "Ma'am, is your son available to play?" The difference in his speech was truly obvious.

One evening when he was about twelve years old, he was asked by a neighbor to watch her two little boys for about two hours while she did her grocery shopping. They lived across the street, and I was home.

These little guys thought he was so cool because he could do wheelies on his bike and run fast. I agreed and was happy that she trusted him and that he'd make a few dollars. The boys were two and four years old. I could hear them playing in the yard for the first hour. After he finished babysitting, he returned home and went to his room to get ready for school the next day. I was just relieved that one of my kids was easy and manageable.

Truly one of the worst evenings of my life was about to occur. An hour later, the mother of these little boys was at my front door. She was hysterical. I had no idea what was going on with her, she could hardly speak. This woman was an attorney and highly respected in the neighborhood. What could be so upsetting to her? She calmed herself enough to tell me in an angry tone that she was just bathing her baby boys and they were excited to show her what my son taught them. He had performed oral sex on each of her children. Then he taught them how to do it to him. Oh my God! My body started to shake. I was frozen and speechless. I didn't know what to say or do. My daughter was home and heard it all. Thank God my older son was out. I went flying up the stairs to his bedroom. I opened the door so violently I almost broke the hinges. He was lying in his bed, playing with a Game Boy.

I screamed at him, begging him to tell me the truth of what happened across the street. I will never forget his calmness. I asked him if it was true what I'd just learned. He nodded his head yes. What the fuck! He didn't even try to deny what he had done. I was screaming, crying, and shaking. *Why! Why! Why?* Why would you do such a thing to these tiny boys? To my absolute disbelief, he very calmly said that people used to do that to him when he was a tiny boy and it felt really good. He said he just wanted these little boys to be happy and feel good too. He truly believed that he was being kind to them.

I couldn't move. I couldn't speak. I was frozen. I was in shock. Oh my God! What do I do now?

The neighbor waited for me downstairs. My daughter was trying to make her feel better. I returned and had to tell her that this *did* occur. Her baby boys were sharing the truth. She screamed. I was so sorry. I held her. I apologized profusely. I did not know how to handle this bizarre scenario. She went flying out the door, running as fast as she could.

Shortly thereafter, a policeman appeared at my door. He had advised her to take the boys to the hospital to be sexually examined by a doctor. Then he told me to immediately bring my son to the police station. Of course, I would do anything to help. I was scared on so many levels.

The two of us walked into the police station. The officer sat him down and did not sugar coat what had happened. He reeled into this kid like he was a dangerous criminal. He asked my son if he had any idea of what he had done and why it was wrong. My son shook his head "no" and told the officer exactly what he had told me. That man looked at me like I had two heads. Of course, I immediately explained that I'd adopted him at age eight and did not know anything about his early childhood. I explained that this was a total shock to me too. The policeman went on to tell him that if he were a few years older, he would be registered as a sexual offender for the rest of his life. He then said to my son that he was damn lucky that the neighbor respected his mother enough and that she would not be pressing charges. However, he had to be brought to the station for the next six weeks for a weekly counseling class on sexual abuse. Not only that, but he was also ordered to write to the parents apologizing for his behavior and he was never permitted to step onto their property again. My son's eyes were full of tears. I will never forget the look on his face. He had absolutely no clue that he had done anything wrong.

I am just thankful for one small detail in this horrendous incident: thank God my other son was not home. I think he would have punished his brother profusely.

Note to self: Not knowing a person's personal history can be like walking on a frozen pond when the sun is shining on it.

Chapter Twenty-One

UP TO THIS POINT, ALL THREE KIDS WERE UNDER MY ROOF. MY older kids' father had retired from the USMC and was remarried. His wife hated the South, so they settled in Pittsburgh where they were both raised. This was of no help to me. They saw the two kids on holidays and for vacations in the summer. Even though he and I always tried to be a united front, I was carrying most of the responsibility. I must admit that although I believed my older son loved no one else in the world like he loved his mom, at this point, I was not successful in raising him alone. He was out of control. I tried everything I knew to do—reason with him, take him to an adolescent counselor, put him on meds, love him with all of my heart. It was useless. He was failing school, drinking, smoking pot, and simply out of control. He would not play any sport or go to church with me.

So, at the age of fourteen, I called his father to say I was putting our son on a plane. I suggested he'd be on the other end waiting for him. I told him that this kid needed a father, and it was time for him to step up. I will never forget how terrified this inexperienced father sounded. He literally said he didn't know how to raise a child. He panicked and said his wife would not be happy. Five hours later, our son was in Pittsburgh. It was not a joyous reunion. But it had to be done.

Our daughter was so distraught over what had occurred with her adopted brother that she applied and was accepted into a high school exchange program. She spent her sixteenth year in Brazil. Although this was an incredible opportunity, I don't believe it was for the right reason. But there was no reasoning with her. Quite frankly, I was exhausted trying. She just wanted to be gone.

This left me alone to raise my adopted son. Selfishly, I welcomed the quiet. I welcomed the peace from not having two unhappy teenagers under my roof. The last few years had been very difficult trying to keep everyone happy and on course. By now, this last child was finishing middle school. He had been very compliant at school and did his chores without complaint. He was truly turning out to be my easiest child. He was immature and not complicated. He and I would spend many evenings watching Disney movies and his favorite show, *Touched by an Angel*. I shook my head smiling, trying to imagine if my other son would ever want to cuddle and watch these sweet, benign shows with his mom. I had a few sweet years with my adopted son.

What I haven't mentioned was how physically talented he was. He couldn't swim when we adopted him. Now he was a fish in the water. He couldn't throw a ball. No one could throw as far as him. He didn't know how to run in a race. Now no one could beat him. But his true love was football. By the time I enrolled him in high school, he was being scouted by the coaches. Although he was not a large kid, he was a natural-born running back. No one could catch him.

He ran through the other players like a ballet dancer on a stage. He was in total control. Football became his life. In fact, he was so good that people always wondered where his family was. A friend of mine had a shirt made for me, saying, "I'm His Mom!"

Because we lived in a neighborhood that was lily-white and whose families were professionals, this particular high school was one of the best in the South. Football is very important in the Deep South. Therefore, I was extra thrilled that I discovered something that this child could do well. All the other players were white boys from affluent homes. Their parents were lawyers, doctors—one was even our mayor. My son was one of the few Black kids in this high school. But as he always did, he won their hearts. The other players loved him. Perhaps they had never really known a Black person, as everything in the South was still highly segregated. Perhaps he was like a mascot to them. Perhaps he was like a new puppy to them, just as he had been with his adopted siblings.

He went to this high school and excelled in football for three years. It offset his lack of academic success. Luckily, he was still being helped by resource teachers to get through each grade. His white football buddies would come to our house often to hang out. I owned a tiny cottage at this point, but I believe these rich boys felt very comfortable lounging in our cozy home. It was not unusual for my son to go to school all day and practice football for hours, and when he got home, I would feed him and we'd both get through his assignments together. Afterward he was free to go out for a few hours with friends. I trusted him far more than I had trusted my first son, who had let me down too many times.

I have reflected on this often. I think it had a lot to do with the level of love I had for my two sons. I would be lying to say it was the same. It wasn't. As any mother knows, birthing a baby from your body provides an attachment that is extremely strong. I discovered that my emotional attachment to my adopted son was very different from my attachment to my first son. Perhaps that is why I had such a difficult time disciplining my older son. I loved him so deeply. He was able to manipulate my love to get what he wanted, whereas my love for my second son was different. It was not as raw. I was able to discipline him without feeling like I was damaging him or upsetting him. Plus, the fact was, he was extremely easy-going and not clever. He didn't play games with my heart. He was a very simple human-being, unlike his siblings, who were complicated and intelligent.

Note to self: Sometimes "simple" is a pleasant change when you're used to dealing with complicated.

Chapter Twenty-One

THE YEARS FLEW BY, AND MY OLDER SON GRADUATED FROM high school in Pittsburgh. Let's just say, he barely graduated. His father and I attended his high school graduation, wondering to the last moment if his name would be called. He had given his dad a rough four years. He never actually broke laws, although the local police in that small town had him on their radar. He was defiant and irresponsible. His dad and his wife separated during those years. His stepmother was the polar opposite of me. He despised her and she resented him. Fortunately for them, they weathered the storm and reunited when he graduated. They remained married for the rest of their life. (Ironically ten years later, his stepmother became his third best fan as an adult, right behind his dad and me.) But after high school graduation the rule was that he had to leave their home. He was fine with that rule. He couldn't wait to get "home." He couldn't get to my house fast enough.

I loved him, so I welcomed him home much like the story of the prodigal son. I erased all the pain of the past. I figured he had to have matured. He had to be more responsible at this age. I even went so far as to get him a summer job with a friend's landscaping company. Now he was gainfully employed the minute he returned. Since he had no college plans, we allowed him to use a portion of the money we'd saved for him to buy a car. His life seemed to be starting off fine. I was thrilled to have him back with me.

I lived in a two-bedroom cottage, so the boys shared a room. I purchased a very cool set of bunk beds with a large futon for their friends. They had their own stereo and cable television in the room. It was a man's cave, and they were happy. My daughter was out of the picture at this time. She had returned from Brazil, finished high school early, and was now away at college. She was still in a bad place with our life and did not choose to visit me very often. She broke my heart so many times during these years, I lost count. Unfortunately, it would be many years before I got any reprieve from her behavior. To this day, I don't know the reason for her deep disdain toward me. I tried to do everything to help her to be successful, and she was. She excelled in every area of her life with my help every step of the way. I believe the cause of her resentments and her emotional distance from me was because of my divorce from her father, my adopting a Black child with serious issues, and my relationships with other men. As I look back on her life, I suppose I would be angry too. Ironically, my mother was a thousand percent tougher to live with, yet all I did was try to love her and make her happy. My daughter needed time away to work through her anger.

Life with a nineteen-year-old son and an eighteen-year-old son buzzed along. They did not hang out with each other. They had different interests and different friends. They seemed to come and go on very different schedules as I stayed home and read books, practiced drawing, and corrected school papers. I did their laundry and made their meals. I know I did too much for them. But it was something I could do and felt good to help them. My life was rather mundane and quiet. I had social dates here and there but no one significant. My older son did not have any friends left in this area since he went to high school in Pittsburgh. When he returned, he began to chum around with the guys from work. Unfortunately, they were not the highest of caliber, academically. None of them had future educational plans. This was disconcerting for me because I had always thought my son would go on to college. Without me knowing it, he began to experiment with harsher drugs. I noticed that he was becoming extremely thin. But in my naivety, I assumed it was from the back-breaking job of landscaping day after day in the Southern sun. That's what I wanted to believe. Talk about denial.

But then it became very clear to me what was going on with him. One evening I went for my debit card. I figured I must have lost it. I called the bank. I was told that someone had withdrawn $200 from an ATM using my card. I was sick. However, I still did not want to believe the worst. My son would never do anything like this to me.

I went to bed distraught. He was not home, but I had to teach school the next day. I had to sleep. At six the next morning, I walked into my small kitchen. There he was on the floor. He was so thin. He was crying so hard. He looked at me and cried, telling me what a loser he was. He could hardly talk; he was so upset. He said he was a piece of shit. His clothes were filthy, and his nose was running down his face. It was one of the darkest moments in my life, looking at him on my kitchen floor. He admitted that he took my card. He also admitted that he got a speeding ticket and that his car was broken down somewhere in a different town. Lastly, he admitted that he had been doing some drugs with his landscaping friends. I wanted to die. I wanted to curl up and die. I had absolutely no idea what to do next. He kept crying and apologizing to me for everything he'd done. He was nineteen and a total mess. I distinctly remember my body shaking. I had no idea what to do. I did not know what to say. I just sat down on the floor next to him, held him, as my body shook.

He agreed to go to the ER with me to be examined. It was truly one of the first times in many years he did what I asked of him. I was so scared I just thought going to the ER was the right thing to do. I needed help and had no one. We waited for hours. When we finally saw a doctor, my son was so ashamed. The doctor knew what was happening. In my ignorance to get help, I asked if he could be admitted. I was scared to take him home. The doctor asked him if he had suicidal thoughts. He said he could only admit him to the hospital if he was in danger of harming himself. I spoke up and said yes, he was. My son looked at me and said he had never once ever thought of suicide. Without much concern or empathy, the doctor simply told him to lay off the drugs and sent us home.

I missed school that day to stay with him. I was terrified to leave him alone. This is a very important point to stress. No matter what is going on in a teacher's personal life...it must always be left at the door so she can fix the other twenty-eight kids in her life. When you walk into the classroom, you better be ready. No one ever knows what teachers are carrying in their hearts. So many young lives are in front of her to fix, no matter what personal hell she might be experiencing. Needless to say, I was not in a good place, and I needed to stay home with my broken son and not try to fix anyone else.

Note to self: Don't give up on him. Believe in him; his core is solid.

Chapter Twenty-Two

IN THE MEANTIME, MY ADOPTED SON WAS OFF FOR THE SUM- mer. I basically ordered him to get a summer job. I made several calls and got him interviews. Again...I did the basic work. He was offered a few menial jobs. He finally agreed to work at the supermarket. He wanted to use my car to drive to work and I told him that he'd have to pay for his own gas and his car insurance, at least until football practice started. I was thrilled that he was earning his own money. I knew that he was doing very well at football, but I was desperately trying to instill responsibility.

We started to receive letters in the mail. Universities were watching him for their football teams. I was astounded to think that these Big Ten schools were serious. The kid hardly made it through eleven years of school. But he was that good! To keep him humble, I downplayed the offers. I remember saying to him that I'd been his momma for ten years now and I had two basic goals in raising him: I needed to keep him safe and alive and to graduate him from high school. Of course, he was more than healthy and alive, but he still had to get through his senior year of high school. I tried to keep his football offers at a low level to keep him humble as well as to guard my other son from feeling like he wasn't as talented. It was a delicate balancing act.

One evening, my older son was out with friends. My second son walked into the cottage with a football buddy. He asked if this buddy could crash on the futon for a few days. He explained that he was in a bad place with his parents and needed a day or so to cool down. I agreed, only if he let his parents know where he was. That young man stayed with us for a week. His parents were grateful, mainly because they weren't sure how to fix what was going on in their home. I asked few questions—I was just happy to help another parent who didn't know what to do. God, I knew how that felt.

About this same time period, I had met a man. He was terribly interested in me. I was less than smitten. However, this man was from England, a country I've always dreamed of living in and truly fantasized about moving to one day. I loved the ridiculous royal gossip and all the pomp and circumstance. Plus, I must admit...his accent was adorable.

He did the perfect thing to get my attention—he literally mailed me handwritten letters, trying to convince me why I should go out with him. Who does that? They were in handwritten script. I have to admit that was probably the smartest gesture he could've done. I am such a romantic at heart. To receive a handwritten love letter in the mail was unheard of in this time of email and texting. He also had a very quirky, yet cute, sense of humor. I think it was less the fact that he was clever and more the fact that he was British through and through. I found his behavior and his humor to be adorable. I was not physically attracted to him, but at that point, I was just thrilled to be getting attention and not having to be the one giving everything to someone else.

With less than a sense of love at first sight, I agreed to date him. He had lots of British friends in town who were very involved in the local "football" team—English football. We spent many hours having entertaining evenings at the semipro soccer games with his British friends and afterward at the pub. For the first time in years, I was having big fun. He treated me like a princess, and I soaked up the attention. I was so starved for someone to love me. He was quite good at soccer and played on a men's league. It was fun to watch him play. It was like living in a foreign culture, hanging out with all of these close-knit Brits. I have to admit that I was not in love with this man, but he made me laugh and I was no longer lonely. Plus, this sure was a wonderful alternative to sitting at home in my cottage worrying about my sons.

What I was to find out later was that he still had four dependent children to raise and financially support, not to mention a very bitter ex-wife who was not about to make anything easy for him. I will always blame the universe for not providing me with a big sister or a wise mother to tell me to "*Run like hell!*" I was so lonely and had no one that I trusted enough to talk to about this situation. In truth, I had no one to blame but myself, because I allowed myself to be talked into this relationship—out of fear. I was terrified about my current state of affairs with my sons. I was terribly lonely and so in need of support and love. I have to believe that too many women find themselves in this position. They are also terrified to be alone for the rest of their lives. We are social creatures. The thought of never being touched, loved, or listened to again was terrifying. Women truly believe that if they find love, no matter how flawed, life will finally be happy. They believe they need a prince to rescue them. This truly is the biggest lie *ever* that we teach our little girls. This is the worst idea to ever put in a young girl's head. Hence, I was about to make yet another *huge* mistake.

We became serious rather quickly; once again, I believe fear drove my decision. Fear is the worst driving force in our lives. So many decisions are made based on fear. This man was extremely kind to me, and more than financial security, I needed emotional security. I allowed him into my lonely life.

One Sunday evening, I had made a lovely dinner for the two of us. Of course, both boys were out. After our dinner, he left to go home as he had his kids for the week. Shortly thereafter, my second son arrived home with a few football buddies. I asked about his workday at the supermarket. But then I noticed he was not wearing the supermarket shirt. He blatantly answered me saying he didn't go to work. I was in shock. I was furious. I asked him how he was planning on paying for gas, insurance, and summer activities. He looked at me and calmly said that he had money and there was plenty more when he needed it. I was confused.. I asked him to explain. I told his buddies they should leave so he and I could talk. With total defiance, he turned, and the group of football players walked out the door. He looked back and said he'd be at his buddy's house, and we could talk tomorrow, and then he was gone.

I settled in for the night in my pajamas, put on my soft classical music to help me calm myself, and made a cup of tea. I had a stack of papers to correct and hoped I could escape my worry by focusing on my work. My stomach was in knots as I sat there reviewing what he had said. He was the son who had always been obedient and easy to live with up to this point. As it was a school night, I got ready for bed. Neither son was home. I tried to text both of them with no success. I simply decided to turn off my brain and go to bed.

It must have been about 1:00 a.m. when my phone rang. It was the police. They said my adopted son's name and asked if I was his mother. When I told them I was, they informed me that I had to retrieve him. He was in the middle of a forest reserve, where apparently these footballers and groupies were having a big drinking party. When the police came to break up this booze party, he took off running through the dark forest. Being drunk, he tripped, and the police informed me that they believed his ankle was broken. I was absolutely furious with that kid. There was a part of me that didn't even want to go get him. Not to mention that I had no idea where this forest was or how to find him.

I called the man I was dating, and he devoutly came to get me, as we drove miles trying to find this place. It was far out in the country in a forest reserve. When we finally found the location, it was close to 4:00 a.m. Police cars were the only lights shining. Parents were pulling up to collect their kids. All white kids with parents in fancy cars. I did not have a fancy car and my son was not white. The police had him in custody. He looked horrible. He was in terrible pain and drunk. I wanted to smack him. I was so angry. We got him into the back seat and made the silent journey home. I decided it was not worth discussing this escapade until the morning. In fact, I was so angry with him, I did not even take him to the ER. I told him to put ice on his ankle and go to bed, and we would deal with it in the morning. I wanted him to suffer a bit. (Probably not the best parenting decision.). We did go to the ER the next morning; where we were told it was fractured and he wouldn't be able to work that summer. I guess his wish had come true. I was disappointed and disgusted. He had really let me down.

If this situation proved anything, I realized that this man in my life was there to support me. Perhaps I needed support more than anything at this time in my life. In a very vulnerable moment, I accepted his proposal and we secretly married. The reason we had to marry was because his wife was extremely uncooperative with him and had the divorce attorney enforce that I was not allowed to be around their kids as a girlfriend of his. But if I was his wife, I certainly was permitted to live in his house with all of them.

We told no one. I stayed at my house, and he stayed at his. However, if I wanted to visit them, there was no reason I couldn't. His three daughters proved to be much like their mother: angry. Unfortunately, I quickly found out that I had, once again, put myself into an unfavorable position. He did have a sweet son who happened to also be a senior at the same high school with my football son. This boy did not cause me any trouble and I was grateful. He was a very shy, slight boy. He was the type of kid I referred to in my classroom as "invisible." These are the children who don't want to be noticed—they want no attention and often were the ones others might bully. He was extremely quiet and hardly looked at me in the face to speak. These timid children were always special to me because they asked for nothing yet needed so much. Interestingly enough, he worked at a smaller local supermarket. He was extremely responsible, reliable, available, and was actually trusted to close the store on Saturday nights when the manager wanted a free night. He had few friends and no social life; therefore, he was perfect for this job.

Note to self: Do not make decisions based on loneliness and fear..

Chapter Twenty-Three

ONE EVENING, MY NEW PARTNER AND I WERE AT MY COTtage. It was about 10 p.m. His phone rang. It was his ex-wife, and she was hysterical. She had just gotten a call from the police to come to the grocery store where their son worked. There had been an armed robbery. He was the person who was robbed by a gun-wielding robber. This poor boy was in shock, frightened to death, and basically cowering in the corner. The robbers got away, and although he was unharmed, he was shaking like a leaf. This kid was only a senior in high school. Of all the kids I'd known who had come through my classroom door, this young man was one of the least equipped to deal with such a traumatic experience. My partner went as quickly as he could to meet them at the police station. By this time, this boy was answering questions and reliving the entire dreadful experience. It was a true nightmare for him. My heart ached for him. He was a good boy. No one deserved such a scare. This boy had a gun aimed directly in his face, and we were terribly worried he'd never be the same.

When my sons came home late that night, I was sitting on the sofa, wide awake. I told them what had happened. They did not know him, but they both listened attentively and agreed how scary it must have been for him. Even though my second son was in the same senior class as this boy, their paths never crossed. He only hung out with the football team.

He was excelling at the game and extremely popular with the other players. College letters were arriving for him to consider their football teams. I was in shock. He was at the top of his game, and I was not only going to get him through high school as I had hoped, but we were now looking at football scholarships. For the first time in a very long time, I felt elated. My job of raising him, keeping him healthy and alive, and getting him through school was all coming to a wonderful conclusion. Soon he'd be playing college football, and I could finally relax and breathe. Although I was still very worried about my older son, he seemed to be in a better place from what I could tell. He didn't have any solid friends yet, but at least he had gained back his weight, and I believed he was living a much healthier life. He continued to work at the landscaping job. He wasn't happy with that job, but it kept his car running. He was a constant concern for me because he just didn't have a future plan.

A few months passed and life was calm. My new husband and I were making our life work the best that we could considering we had seven teenagers between us. His girls continued to be difficult, so I kept my distance as much as possible. It certainly was not an ideal marriage. As I look back at it, I must have had such low self-esteem to agree to this arrangement. Loneliness can be a vicious companion. It deceives you and leads you astray. How I wished I had more confidence to live my life alone. My daughter was certainly not happy with this new partner of mine. She thought he was far below my intellect and standards. This gave her one more reason to stay away and be cross with me. Sigh.

But in her defense, she was excelling. She had graduated from college with honors. She'd taken the LSAT exam and had a solid score. She applied to only two law schools and was immediately accepted at both. Of course, the schools she chose were as far from Charleston as possible. Her ultimate choice was a law school in the Northwest. I actually had to look at the map of the USA to know exactly where they were located. Needless to say, both were thousands of miles away. I was proud of her accomplishments but brokenhearted that she was going to be so far away. Plus, if she went to law school out in the Northwest, she would take the bar exam there and make a life out there too. She had spent every summer in college working at Yellowstone Park. She fell in love with the West. She had never been comfortable in the Deep South where she was raised. But I had never been comfortable with where I had been raised either. So, I suppose I shouldn't have been surprised that she would do the same as I did. It just broke my heart that my only daughter, the pride of my life, up to this point, wanted nothing to do with me, and didn't see any of the good that I was. My prayer was that time will heal our relationship.

One evening after I made dinner for my boys and me, they went out with different friends. I settled into my routine of preparing lesson plans for the week and getting lunches packed for the three of us. I enjoyed this time of day because I was alone and feeling satisfied that life was progressing nicely. About 9:00 p.m., there was a knock—no, it was more like a pounding—on my front door. It startled me. When I opened the door, I was faced with several policemen. Their lights were flashing on their police cars. I was scared. I feared something horrible had happened to one of my boys.

However, I instantly realized that the police did not have looks of sympathy or empathy on their faces. They looked serious and angry. My first thought was that my older son, who was still vulnerable, might be in trouble. The policemen pushed their way into my living room without invitation. They had a search warrant. They were rude to me as they ordered me to sit down and stay out of the way. What the hell was happening! They started opening closets, drawers, anything they could grab. They asked me where my sons slept. I pointed to their room. They went crazy in there. They pulled everything out of the drawers and the closet. I had done the boys' laundry earlier that day and their clean, folded clothes were sitting on their respective beds. I didn't mind doing their laundry, but the least they could do was put it away themselves. There was no reason for me to look through their drawers. They were almost grown.

Within minutes, the officer in charge walked over to me and screamed at me. He asked me if I was trying to cover for my son by not calling them. I was absolutely baffled by his question. What son? What was I hiding? What was happening? The other policemen came out of their bedroom wearing gloves and carrying several evidence bags of items. I still did not know what was transpiring. I started to cry, asking them to explain and stop yelling at me. They said my adopted son's name and asked me if I was his mother. OMG! I never expected them to say *his* name. I truly was preparing myself to hear my older son's name.

To this day I will never forget their words. They asked me what kind of mother I was that I didn't know what was in his drawers. I told them I don't go through their drawers. I respected their privacy. They put their own clothes away.

It is difficult to write this next paragraph. I will probably never get over this horrendous moment in my life. There have been times throughout my fifty-plus years that I've truly wanted to give up and die. But nothing was as profound as this moment.

In his underwear drawer, the police found a black ski mask, black gloves, a black hoodie, a paintball gun identical to a pistol, paintballs, a bag of pot, and car keys to a BMW and several hundred dollars. *Breathe. Just breathe! This can't be happening!*

He was being arrested for robbing the supermarket that my husband's son was managing on that dreadful night. *My son robbed his son!* My son terrified that sweet boy, literally his own stepbrother. But the most frightening part of all of this was that my son never led on to knowing anything about that robbery. He never even showed a morsel of guilt. He simply went about his life living in my house, allowing me to take care of his every need. He just took and took from me, and I allowed it, thinking that was my job as his adoptive mother.

I felt like I was going to have a nervous breakdown. My entire body was shaking. They did not care how I was or that I was shaking and crying. They ordered me to tell them where he was. I told them that he had gone out with his football friends to one of their houses, where they were playing video games. The police handed my phone to me, ordering me to call him, which I did. He answered my call. As clearly and calmly as possible, with a room full of police watching me, I asked him specifically where he was. I was not permitted to say anything else. My son told me the boy's address, where they were hanging out playing football video games. Within seconds, the police were racing away from my house toward the house where the boys were. The sirens were blaring, and the lights were flashing.

My life would never, ever be the same again. I stood in my small cottage and screamed in horror of what was happening.

The police quickly found the house. It was in an affluent neighborhood. The entire basement was a recreation room for the kids. There were twelve football players hanging out when the police busted into the house. The parents were upstairs and had no idea of what was happening. All twelve boys were questioned and arrested. Parents were called and the boys were taken to the police station.

It was disclosed that these twelve senior football players came up with a plan to get fast, easy money. The plan was to steal a car and rob the supermarket, as well as a Subway sandwich store. They wanted money, so one of the boys, who had stayed at my house, could run away from his parents, whom he hated. Such entitled, spoiled kids. These boys actually planned all of this together. My son was the only Black kid. He was the one who they *all* agreed would go into the stores to do the robbing. The others would sit outside in the cars watching and speed away afterward. Why him? Was it because he was Black? Or was it because he was just stupid?

There are so many parts of this entire nightmare that I will *never* understand:

1. How did the police know to come to my house?
2. What would ever make these successful football players, from wealthy homes, commit such horrific crimes?
3. How could they have ever thought they'd get away with these crimes?
4. Why would they think that this was OK to do, with all twelve of them agreeing?
5. How could my son do such horrible acts after the last ten years of teaching and modeling positive social and moral behavior?

Perhaps this is called "herd mentality," but in my mind, it was just plain wrong on every level. I was never so hurt, disappointed, and more than anything, frightened.

The boys were booked into the county jail for the night. The wealthy parents were demanding to get them out. But they were required to stay until the arraignment. The arraignment would be the following morning.

They were permitted to make one phone call. Of course, my son called me. I did not answer the phone. I sat alone in the darkness of my disheveled home. I was so terribly angry. I could hardly breathe or think straight. How dare he call me? What did he want me to say? What could I possibly do for him now?

After slowing my breathing and stopping my crying, I called the man I had just married. How could I even begin to tell him what had happened?

He came rushing over to my house. He hugged me as I sobbed. Then I called my older son. When my older son walked into the cottage to see the mess, he was furious. It looked as though the house had been looted. He could not calm himself down once he heard what his brother had done. He was in shock. He told me that he had seen BMW keys on his brother's dresser, but he assumed they were from one of the rich kids' parent's cars. He never thought twice about it. He was floored that he shared a room with this person who could do all of this and go to sleep peacefully night after night. These crimes happened months ago. He had slept in the same room with this criminal for months. If ever my older son had regretted the adoption, he had kept it to himself. Now things were very different. He had shared everything with his brother since I brought him home ten years ago. He had watched me spend hours helping his brother instead of spending time with him. I have never seen my older son so angry. I am just glad the police had his brother at the county jail, for I fear it would have been a very scary situation if he had been home.

I didn't realize at this time that this was the very beginning of the end of this marriage. Our kids would eventually destroy any happiness we had with each other. This horrible episode was only the beginning. But I must give this man, whom I married, massive amounts of credit. He came to me knowing that my son had absolutely traumatized his own flesh and blood. Yet, he was very kind to me. He knew I was nothing but a witness to this horrendous situation. He never once passed judgement. He totally supported me. I will always be grateful in my heart for how I was treated that night. He showed unconditional love even though his sweet son was the victim of my son's crime.

The next day, my older son and I went to the arraignment at the county courthouse. All twelve boys were in handcuffs, standing in a line. It was surreal. My husband chose not to be there out of respect for me. His ex-wife sat with their son in the courtroom. She was not on good terms with her ex-husband and seeing him there would only escalate the situation.

The judge explained that not only did these football players traumatize his son, but also that the young woman working at the Subway, that they robbed, was pregnant. She was so frightened that she fainted. She was taken to the hospital by ambulance and thankfully did not lose her baby. If she had lost her baby, there would be murder charges too. Unbelievable! A baby! Oh, dear God!

The BMW belonged to a random man who lived in a lovely neighborhood. Most of these boys came from affluent families. One of the boys knew that this man never locked his car door and left his keys in it because it was a gated community. They were neighbors. The tears of total disbelief just poured down my face. My older son just stared, stone-faced. Then it ended. There was total silence. I didn't know what to do or say. I felt like a horrible mother because I had a son who would do such crimes.

The boys were taken back into the jail holding cells. Bail had been set at $500,000 each. The other parents had the money to bail out their sons. I didn't. Even if I'd had that money, I wouldn't have bailed him out of this mess immediately. I had never felt so used, betrayed, disrespected, and abused in my life. He had taken absolute advantage of my kindness toward him. In my opinion, he needed to sit there and reflect on how many people he had hurt. How many families he had destroyed. How deceitful he had been.

As life would have it, I was planning to leave on a trip, the very next day, with my daughter. We were flying to Tuscany, Italy. A childhood friend of mine had rented a villa for a month and invited us to visit at no cost for the entire week. This trip was to congratulate my daughter on graduating from the university with honors and being accepted into a prestigious law school. My hope was that this trip would be a healing experience for the two of us. The airline tickets were nonrefundable. Not only would I lose the money for these tickets, but I'd have to use them in the next year to go to Tuscany. We were to be gone one week. There would not be another opportunity to revisit Tuscany in this next year. There would be no easy way to explain this to her. Once again, she would have to take a backseat to her adopted brother who has needed so much of my time in the last ten years. This would certainly not add to the healing of our personal relationship.

Once again, I had to make a very difficult decision on whether to stay home and find the money to bail him out of jail or to go on this trip. Finally, I made up my mind that he should sit in the county jail for a week, and I would deal with him when I returned. It was totally unfair to cancel this gift that my daughter had earned by doing all the right things. It was probably one of the most difficult decisions of my lifetime up to this point. But it was time to put her first.

We left, and he remained in the county jail. All the other boys got bailed out. Unbeknownst to me, one of the wealthy fathers took it upon themselves to bail out *my* son. He did not contact me. They all felt sorry for him that I was on a European trip, and I just left him sitting in jail. Someone actually called the local newspaper to do a story on these crimes. In that article, I was described as a heartless jetsetter who didn't care about this poor, confused child.

My older son emailed me three days into our trip. He told me his brother was back at home. He told me he wanted to use my car, but he hid my keys. He told me that his buddies were there, discussing what was going to happen. He said these boys were not a bit upset or worried. Two of their fathers were successful attorneys and the others had money to hire high-end defense attorneys. They knew they'd only get a slap on the hand. He said they sat around discussing the different universities that wanted them to play football. I tried desperately not to let all of this ruin my daughter's trip. She had sacrificed so much of her life for this kid since I'd brought him home ten years ago. I'd deal with it when I got home. Needless to say, I had a horrible time, but tried not to show it. I tried to smile for her.

When I got home, both boys were at the house. I looked at my adopted son in total disbelief. All I could say was, "What the hell were you thinking to do such things?" He shrugged his shoulders. He had nothing to say. My eyes were streaming with angry tears. I told him to get out of my house. He was eighteen and I just wanted him gone. I was done. I was so done! Get out. I didn't care where he went.

He left and jumped into a sports car with a football friend. I went crazy. I packed all of his clothes, shoes, everything in his drawers, and threw the boxes and bags into the front yard. Then I sent my older son to the hardware store to buy deadbolt locks for the two doors. There was no way I was going to allow this grown man to live under my roof any longer. If he had such wealthy friends, let them give him a place to stay. How could I ever feel safe again when he had a gun, bullets, ski masks, gloves, black hoodies, stolen car keys, cash, and pot in my house for the last several months? Then, when I checked the store where I had gotten him a summer job, I found out that he never showed up for the job. He used my car all summer to go to work. He lied to me about working, without even blinking his eyes. It was all so heartbreaking and terrifying.

Summer passed and I had to return to school and face everyone. Yes...Miss Teacher of the Year! What kind of teacher has a kid who does these horrible things? I hung my head. I was so ashamed. Of course, everyone was kind. No matter what they were actually thinking, no one punished me for what he had done. One teacher, who had a son who was also a senior at the same high school, took me in her arms with tears and said, "Only by the grace of God am I spared."

Even my students' parents showed much love and compassion toward me. Most people were sick over the whole mess. It was the talk of this large community. No one could believe these successful football players from such good families would commit such unimaginable crimes. I know my colleagues wished they could do something to help me. It took every inch of emotional, mental, and physical strength to show up each day to teach. As they say, the show must go on. Teachers must worry about everyone else's child when at work and leave their own problems at the door.

Note to self: Sometimes having to be at
work is a blessing in disguise.

Chapter Twenty-Four

SHORTLY AFTER GETTING BACK TO SCHOOL, I BEGAN TO REALLY suffer with lower back pain. This seemed unusual, as I normally didn't have backaches. I figured it was due to all of the stress I was enduring. But with each day, the pain increased. My teacher friends teased me, telling me I just needed more fiber in my life. They were all so gentle with me, knowing how fragile my heart was. They even bought me a jar of Metamucil and put a bow around the container. They knew my nerves were shot. They tried to make light of everything so I could try to smile again. After a week of truly suffering, it was getting worse. I taught all day and then drove myself straight to the ER at the large hospital downtown. As I was waiting to be seen, I was terribly cold. I started to uncontrollably shiver. A nurse saw me and led me to a room. My temperature was 104°F. The doctor immediately informed me that I needed to be admitted. I was burning up with fever, which meant there was a serious infection attacking my body. I told them that my lower back was extremely painful.

I had no idea, but I had been carrying a serious kidney infection for over a week. I was not aware as I had never had one before. Unfortunately, my body became septic. The infection had spread throughout my bloodstream. The doctors and nurses worked as quickly as they could. I am allergic to penicillin, sulfa drugs, and a few other powerful medications, so they had to put their heads together. By now, I was in and out of consciousness. One of the young doctors held my hand and asked me who they could call. This sweet, compassionate professional explained that this was very serious. They wanted my family here as quickly as possible. It was only at that moment that I realized how deathly ill I was. From what I could understand, I must have had a UTI that went untreated. Then, it spread to my bladder, my kidneys, and now throughout my bloodstream. I was so sick; it was difficult to think or speak. I was able to give them my husband's number as well as my older son's number.

Within an hour, they were both in my room. My son was terribly upset. He started to cry. Even though his teenage years had been difficult, he loved me with all of his heart, and I knew it. I just continued to pray for him to find his way. At nineteen, he was not a crier. Seeing him in tears was frightening. My deplorable condition truly scared him. He really had never seen me sick. I was always there for everyone, holding it together. I never allowed myself to be ill.

I will never forget the image of him sitting on the bottom of my hospital bed, holding his head in his hands as he softly cried. After a while, he came to me and whispered in my ear. He said he was so sorry for all the pain and heartbreak he had caused me growing up. He promised that if I recovered, he would make me proud for the rest of my life and his. He said he was done being a loser and it was time for him to step up. Then he laid his head on my shoulder and begged me to be OK. I couldn't even open my eyes, but I heard his words and tried to smile to ease his pain.

My husband sat next to my bed, holding my hand for hours. I finally woke up and whispered that I was so sick and wasn't sure I'd be able to recover. I begged him to help my older son get over this and let my daughter know that she should come to see me. She was away at law school. As far as my younger son was concerned, I was too sick and sad to know what to suggest.

Three very rough days went by, but my body finally turned the corner. The medications did their job and fought the infection. As I opened my eyes on that third day, I saw my older son sitting next to my bed. He was holding one rose. When he realized that I was awake, he jumped up to kiss my cheek. He handed me the rose and told me he had really good news to tell me. He explained that he joined the Army. He said he was starting from the bottom but was going to climb as high as he could go. He explained that the Army would teach him a skill that he could use someday. He also said he was leaving for boot camp in two weeks. At nineteen years old, he had a plan. I cried hearing the news. To be honest, I'm not sure if I cried out of fear for what he was about to do, out of happiness for him that he finally had a future plan, or simply from feeling absolute, total *relief*.

Note to self: Never take your good health for granted.

Chapter Twenty-Five

THE TRIAL WAS SET SIX MONTHS AFTER THE ARREST. MY SON had a public defender. The other boys had expensive, powerful attorneys. He continued to live with one of the wealthy boys involved in the crime. I heard that during this time, the boys continued to drink and smoke pot. They were all at a party with no adult supervision and were arrested again. He was halfway through his senior year when that happened.

I did not attend the trial. I couldn't fathom sitting through it. My husband went to support his son who had been so badly victimized by these boys. The judge scolded these boys profusely. He told them that they had a chance to get straight and show remorse but continued to party even while waiting for this trial. But because of their clever attorneys, they received not much more than a slap on the wrist. He gave eleven of the group six weeks at a boot camp for juveniles. Their attorneys argued that all they did was sit in the cars and watch. They were all seventeen years old, and still immature children. They should not be severely punished. Disgusting.

My son was the one holding the gun in the faces of the two victims. It turned out to be an inexpensive paintball gun, but it looked like a real pistol. In the state of South Carolina, if you use a toy gun or anything that resembles a gun for a crime, it is considered armed robbery. The stolen car was driven by my son also. Grand theft. The pot was found in his drawer. Illegal drugs. The ski mask, gloves, and black clothes were in his drawers and not any of the other's drawers. He was eighteen years old. He was considered an adult, which now made him a felon. Might I mention once more that he was the only Black boy? I will always wonder if that contributed to his sentence.

The judge sentenced him to ten years in a South Carolina adult male penitentiary. Ten years! They took him straight to the prison after the trial. The other boys were permitted to finish their senior year of high school and do their boot camp during the summer.

I had no way to reach him. I wasn't even sure where they took him. I heard they often sent prisoners to different facilities initially to find the best fit. I did not see him for a long time after that horrible day. I did not hear from him or anyone else concerning his well-being. Plus, I had no one to call. They shaved his head, gave him orange prison clothes, and locked him in a cell for the next ten years of his life, and no one seemed to care but me.

All I ever wanted was for him to stay alive, be healthy, and graduate from high school. He was healthy, but he never graduated. He was two-thirds of the way through his senior year when he went to prison. He never played football again. All the university letters stopped coming. His life was over as he had known it. This story might slightly remind you of the popular movie entitled *Blindside* with Sandra Bullock. In the movie, a pretty white Southern woman adopted a Black football player who did not have a home. He went on to play in the NFL. My story is similar and could have had a happy plot. Unfortunately, my story had a very different ending.

My son was given every opportunity to rise above the desolate scenario of which he'd been born. He made choices that absolutely unraveled everything I had tried to give him. He ruined the family that had taken him in ten years earlier. His adopted siblings would have nothing to do with him. They were angry, embarrassed, humiliated, and in shock. What he did to my heart cannot be explained. I will always carry a broken piece of him, but I'm not sure it will ever heal. Ever. I wasted ten years of my life trying to be a miracle worker.

When The Beatles had their hit song, *"All You Need Is Love,"* everyone believed that love could heal all wounds. Everyone thought that love was the one thing needed to fix any problem. I will never listen to that song again without changing the station. It's a total misconception to think that love can heal all. There is so much more needed than *love*. My good intentions of helping this little lost soul by nurturing and loving him were for not. I should have never thought I could save him. He would have survived on the streets. Now he is exactly where he had been destined to be before I thought I could provide a small miracle. It was wrong of me to believe that I could save this kid simply by loving him. I had failed. Love was certainly not enough.

Note to self: You alone cannot save the world!

Chapter Twenty-Six

NOW I WAS ALONE IN THE COTTAGE. THERE WAS NO NEED TO keep it. None of my kids would be coming home to live. My daughter was deep into law school out West. My older son was stationed in Germany. He was being deployed to Iraq within a few months. My younger son was locked up for a decade. My husband asked me to move in with him and his three daughters. It made sense. So, I sold the cottage and joined his family. It was time to be with him and try to make this marriage work. He had been nothing but kind to me throughout this last horrible year. With great hope, I moved in with them. I gave it everything I had.

People can be nice to your face, but I learned not to believe a lot of people who claimed to be my friend. Judgement is a horrible destroyer of the soul. This was my third marriage. My own brothers teased me unmercifully about being on my third marriage. Three's a charm! Maybe you'll get it right this time! It was cruel, but I guess they thought they were being funny. I suppose I deserved it. Not many people got married three times. The entire time I was going through absolute hell with my son, they didn't contact me to talk, to help, or to care. It was obvious that they thought I was crazy to have done what I did, adopting a Black child. Perhaps they were right. I'm sure they shook their heads at me.

My college friends kept their distance. I'm sure they were all busy in their own lives. But I felt that I was the subject of gossip. I was on my third marriage and had a son in prison. Now that does provide some juicy scoop. Sadly, few of those friends reached out to me. I'd like to think they just didn't know what to say or do.

However, it is important to mention that my very first childhood friend was there if I needed her. She and her husband were financially set, and I knew in my heart that if I was ever in dire need of funds, they would help me. I will never forget her sending me my first laptop computer because I didn't own one. She was generous and kind to me. Although we didn't have many things in common throughout our adult lives, our childhood bond remained strong. I will always be grateful to her for her unwavering love and support. She did not judge my life's decisions.

There is one other person who was a guardian angel to me. I have a cousin who acted very much like a big brother to me. He was at least eighteen years my senior. But he took me under his wing. He seemed to know that the world was not being kind to me. He wrote to me often, offering uplifting advice. I will never forget his generosity when he sent me money to help get my son started once he was out of prison. This man never asked for anything from me. He only tried to ease my struggle. He was one of my heroes on this planet.

Note to self: Never forget to pay it forward...in their honor.

Chapter Twenty-Seven

DURING THIS SHORT TIME OF BEING WITH THIS MAN AND HIS daughters, my dad passed. I kept the heartache of what I was experiencing from my dad. He never knew about my son being in prison. It took him years to accept my Black son. He was horrified that I would adopt a "colored kid" and didn't speak to me for six months when I first brought him home to live with us. Over the next ten years, Dad slowly got to know him. Very slowly, he saw this child as a little boy, not just as a Black child. My son adored my dad. He would climb onto his lap and snuggle. He knew Dad loved to golf, so he would go to the nearby golf course to find lost golf balls for him. I secretly smiled to see my prejudiced father holding my "colored kid." With time, Dad actually started to give him presents like my other two children. He was truly proud of his football success. Dad had a wonderful seventeen years with his lady friend after Mom died. He has been very happy. I was not going to cause him any concern or angst by sharing my sad news.

One autumn day in September, dad fainted on the golf course. We thought he had a heart attack. When they got him to the hospital, they found that his body was riddled with cancer. Ironically, he was such a strong, healthy man, he had no idea that he was sick. His lady friend asked to take care of him. She refused to bring in a caretaker. For three painful months, she was his caretaker, cook, housekeeper, and confidant. Because of her kindness, we didn't have to interrupt our daily lives to care for him. She loved him and was amazingly kind to him. But by Christmas, three months later, Dad was dead. The cancer took him down quickly. I couldn't believe how fast he died. The strangest part of all of this is that he died on Christmas Eve, exactly as my mom had died seventeen years earlier. I will always believe that was not a coincidence. What are the chances of that happening? Unfortunately, Christmas Eve will never be a joyful day for me.

Of course, he had appointed my older brother to be the executor of the will. After his death, his precious lady friend came to me and said that she wanted nothing from Dad's home or the Florida condo. She simply asked me if she could have Dad's car because of all the beautiful memories of driving from Pennsylvania to Florida and back for the last seventeen years. They had so many happy hours in that car. I thought that was a wonderful idea. I was very impressed with her not having any desire to ask for anything else. She had seventeen wonderful years with him. That's all she wanted.

When I went to my two brothers to make this happen, I was astounded to hear their reaction to the request. They said *no*! They said if dad wanted her to have that car, he would've put it in his will. I looked at them like they were out of their minds. This humble and kind lady had loved our dad and cared for him, so we didn't have to interrupt our own lives. How could they possibly say no to her?

I wept. I could not believe their heartlessness. I had to tell this sweet woman that it was out of my control. She looked at me with deep sadness. Then she quietly told me that none of us would ever hear from her again. I hugged her and I apologized on behalf of my brothers. She said she understood my position. However, her hurt was deep. She quietly walked away. I have never forgiven my brothers for their lack of empathy toward this sweet woman. Maybe they believed it would have been disrespectful to our mother. I tried to see their position. I just wanted to thank her for loving our dad.

They ended up selling the car. I told them I wanted no proceeds from that sale. I never heard from her again. But a year later, someone sent me the obituary of her death that was in the newspaper. I was never able to properly thank her or pay her respects.

Why do I share this? Because my third marriage didn't last. I alluded to this earlier. So once again, I found myself in a position of ridicule from my brothers and others. Maybe they had every right to find fault with my life decisions. But at this point, I quit caring what they thought. Perhaps that is why they never took my requests seriously. It was obvious that they did not respect me, love me, or want to help me. I had to come to terms with these facts.

It turned out that my husband's three daughters behaved horribly. They disliked me from day one. There were pregnancies, abortions, alcoholism, drugs, theft. They had so many problems. I did not have the strength nor desire to take on the job of "fixing" them. Plus, I was seeing the small profit from the sale of my cottage being used to help my husband bail them out of different situations. I couldn't do it anymore. I couldn't suffer anymore. Those girls made our union so miserable that I had to leave. My husband understood that there was no fixing this. We had made a huge mistake to think this marriage would ever be successful, let alone happy. In one of the darkest moments of my life, I walked away from that marriage. We parted ways as dear friends, knowing that we had hoped to make a silk purse out of a sow's ear. It would never be possible. And once again, I provided the people I thought were my family and closest friends more reasons to judge me unmercifully.

I have always loved Bob Seger's music. But none of his songs meant as much to me as this song, "Roll Me Away." In this song, he talks about being sick of his own voice. So, he jumped on a huge motorcycle and rode for hundreds of miles to escape his reality. At one point, he stopped in a bar for a brew. He met a woman who asked him what he was going to do. She looked out the window as he spoke. Then she turned to look into his eyes, and he knew what she was thinking. These words were exactly what I was living. He sang, *"Roll me away, won't you roll me away tonight? I, too, am lost, I feel double-crossed, and I'm sick of what is wrong and what's right."* Then these two strangers walked out into the night and rode away, with no plan or destination. I've often dreamed that I could just disappear. I wished I could jump on a train with a one-way ticket and never come back. At this point in my life, I was exhausted in every part of my person. I had no more to give to anyone. In my very sad mind, there was nothing to look forward to and no reason to continue.

Note to self: Pulling inward in your cocoon is sometimes necessary in order to survive the pain.

Chapter Twenty-Eight

TWO LONG AND LONELY YEARS AFTER MY SON WAS SENT TO prison, my phone rang one night after midnight. It startled me, but at least not like years before when I had wild teenagers. I figured it was a misdial. I could not think of anyone who would call me at this hour.

When I answered the phone, all I heard was the word "Mom." It was a man's voice. It could not be my son calling from Iraq—that was not possible. But how could it be my son in prison? To my greatest surprise, it was him. He said his name. I was floored. I didn't know what to say or how to react.

Apparently, he had confiscated an illegal cell phone somehow. He didn't have much time to talk; he had to dispose of it. After more than two years of not hearing from him, he said, "Mom, I'm sorry." Then there was a long pause. "Mom, please help me." Again, a pause. Then he said what I've prayed for so long. He said, "Mom, I love you." He told me that the only way for me to help him was to put a few dollars into his prison account. He had no idea how that worked, but I told him I'd figure it out and send some money. Then he invited me to visit him. He said he hadn't put my name on his visitor's list for over two years because he was angry at me. But he'd had a lot of time to think.

He asked me to come on Saturday for an hour to see him. He said he needed to see me and to talk. He was truly suffering, and he needed his mom. Ironically, he had listed the other boys' names on his visitor's list. Not one had come to see him. What was really happening?

I have never dealt with prisons. I had no idea what to do to send him money. Finally, after researching it, I found that I could send about $100 a month to help him buy toiletries, snacks, warm socks, pencils, paper, envelopes, and stamps. He would not see the money; he could only subtract from the account I set up for him. Then, I googled to see where his prison was located. It was two and a half hours away from my home. What an experience I was about to have. Never in my wildest dreams would I think I'd be going to a prison to visit someone. I was terrified at what lay ahead.

The following Saturday, I begin my trek to the penitentiary. After two and a half anxious hours, I pulled into a very barren parking lot with towers surrounding it. When you visit an inmate, you wait outside a gate. You can have absolutely nothing with you except your car keys, but they are immediately taken from you and secured. No purses, no books, no bags, no photos...nothing was allowed into the prison. One by one, the family members waited to be allowed into the first room. I was the only Caucasian. I was truly out of my element. I was terribly out of my comfort zone. Plus, I was scared. It was intimidating and aesthetically ugly in every way. I waited my turn, patiently wishing I was anywhere but there.

My thought was to dress professionally. I had decided to wear a smart skirt and a tailored blouse. When I got to the room to be checked and examined, the female guard stopped and stared at me. Then in an annoyed tone, she asked me why I was dressed for the office. I did not understand her question. With a sigh, she told me that I could not enter the prison. I was dressed inappropriately. I was told that I needed to wear sweatpants and a sweatshirt or hospital scrubs. I was to wear tennis shoes and socks. I was not to wear makeup or style my hair. A ponytail was sufficient. Then, just like that, she dismissed me and sent me away. She told me to try again next Saturday—and not to wear any jewelry.

I had driven over two and a half hours to a horrific place only to be sent away. My son was going to think I didn't come. I had no way of letting him know that I had tried. Unbelievable. The guard told me that in this all-male prison, I would not be safe dressed as I was. Even if men couldn't get to me, it would excite them, and they would be wild. Prison riots began in manners such as this. Are you kidding? I'm a middle-aged elementary teacher, not Marilyn Monroe.

All week, I felt sad that he was probably thinking he'd been abandoned once more in his life, but this was out of my hands. I went to Walmart after school one day and bought sweatpants and a sweatshirt. I never wear these types of big, loose clothes, so I felt very frumpy. This was certainly not my style. The following Saturday, I made that long, lonely drive again. I looked so plain and totally unattractive. But I guess that's the whole idea.

When I got to the first room, I was examined, and my keys were taken. The guard used her phone to call the prison, requesting that inmate 654321 be sent to the visitor's room. Then I was sent to the next locked gate. At that gate there was another guard, who checked to ensure that I had nothing on my person. The gate opened and I was told to walk to a specific door. It was terrifying because of all the barbed wire and armed guards surrounding me. I could see inmates up on floors with bars on the windows. I had to walk across a long prison yard to that gate. I heard inappropriate comments and howls. I had never felt more vulnerable in my life. When I reached the locked door, I had to press a button. A guard opened the door and asked me who I was here to see. After telling him my son's number, I was allowed to enter a very desolate room. It contained a half dozen horrible old metal tables with chairs opposite each other. I was told where to sit, facing a certain direction with my two hands on the table.

About twenty minutes later, I heard a door open. I looked up. There he was. I hardly recognized him. He was over twenty years old now. He had grown taller and had a lot more body hair. His head was shaved but his arms were covered in hair. His head was covered with psoriasis. It looked like an insect had dug tunnels over his head through his black scalp. I didn't know this person. The only thing I recognized was his gorgeous teeth.

A guard directed him to sit opposite of me. I couldn't help but start to get choked up. I had not seen his face in over two and a half years. I reached out to touch him, to hug him, but was quickly reprimanded by the guard that there was absolutely no physical contact.

He smiled sweetly at me and told me he was really glad I came. I immediately told him that I had tried last week and what had happened. He smiled and said he had never seen me in sweats. He had lost his beautiful articulation and spoke with a "ghetto" twang. I asked him about his speech, not as a criticism but more out of curiosity. He told me when he first came to the prison, he got roughed-up pretty badly for sounding like a white person. He said he had to adapt his speech. He said he had to learn how to be Black again. Poor kid.

I did most of the talking. Actually, I did all of the talking. I told him about his brother in Iraq. His brother was kicking down doors, searching houses. He was stationed there during the time that *American Sniper* was written, and he was not the famous sniper hero. He was one of the low-ranking grunts who kicked in the doors, looking for bad guys. It was terribly dangerous, with no glory given to him as was given to Chris Kyle. He listened attentively. He was very proud of his brother.

I told him about his sister finishing law school. She was going to live out West and begin her professional life as a lawyer. Her future looked very bright as a lawyer. She did well.

I told him that I was getting closer to retirement with only a handful of years left. I also told him that his grandfather, my dad, had died.

It is truly a challenge to keep a conversation going when the other person has nothing to contribute. Since I couldn't bring any photos, news articles, or any prompts at all, I had to be prepared in my mind to keep the conversation going. He had little to tell me. I've never been a person comfortable with silence between two people. So, I found myself babbling nonsensically. After that, as my visits continued, I was carefully listening to every news station I could just to have things to discuss.

Ironically, he did say that not one of the eleven boys had written to him or visited him in the last two years since he was imprisoned. Not one! Isn't that just incredible that they had been his total life? The sacrifices he had made to prove he was part of that elite football group...he even had a girlfriend during that time, who had not even written him a letter, let alone visited him. Now he was totally alone. How very sad, but I was not the least bit surprised. I sat there thinking, *if he had only listened to me back then.* But now it was too late. He had eight more years left in his sentence. Eight more years in this hellhole. Eternity.

I continued to visit him once a month for the next six and a half years. Every visit was difficult for me as I had to talk endlessly about anything I had read or heard with little to no feedback. For six and a half years, he contributed nothing, he just listened. The biggest joy of my visits was when I was allowed to buy him something out of the old vending machines. He was not permitted to touch the vending machines. I had to do it for him. I could only use a card, no money. The card had to be purchased at the guard office when I first entered. I can still smell the horrible odor of a packaged hamburger coming out of a vending machine. I dreaded the Saturday each month that I had to go to the prison. It was a whole day excursion and totally unfulfilling. But he lived for my visits. I was still his mother.

I tutored after school several times a week for hours. I had to start putting money away for his release. As a teacher, I lived pretty much paycheck to paycheck. Therefore, I had to get another job to earn money for him. Tutoring was the best way for me to accomplish this task. But that meant teaching all day and then tutoring for three additional hours after school. It was exhausting. I was putting money away to help him get started when he was released. Plus, I was sending him $100 a month for miscellaneous items as well as making that trip once a month. I knew he'd need a car, a job, clothes, and a place to stay, just to mention the basics needed. The full list of necessities was overwhelming.

My other two kids have no idea how much money it took to get him back on his feet. They didn't need to know. They seldom ask me about him. They had washed their hands of him. I understood their anger, but I was in a tough position. I couldn't talk to them about him. But he had no one else on the planet to help him.

Note to self: When you are called to help someone, find it in your heart to help ease their struggle without dangerously impacting your own life.

Chapter Twenty-Nine

BECAUSE OF GOOD BEHAVIOR, HE WAS RELEASED AT EIGHT and a half years instead of ten years. It was right before his 27th birthday. He had been behind bars for eight and a half years! He had missed all of the technological changes during those years. He would be clueless about most things when he was released. He had spent the majority of his twenties in prison. Take a moment to think about how much a person grows during that decade of life. Think about the changes, career decisions, relationship experiences, geographical moves, and just plain maturity that occurs during one's twenties. None of that had happened in his life. He had been in a time vacuum for eight and a half years. He had been stagnant. I had been his only visitor, and I certainly wasn't the hippest person to teach him about all the new apps and technology.

Upon his release, the prison gave him a one-way bus ticket to travel anywhere in the state. He was allowed to get a set of clothes from the prison's charity clothes closet, so he'd have something to wear on the bus. They gave him $10 to eat once he got to his destination. Nothing more.

I could write an entire book on what I experienced in helping him to reenter society. I should record what I had to do to get him settled. Perhaps it could be of help to others trying to help a newly released felon. It was hours, days, weeks of effort, time, money, and frustration. It is very clear to me why many felons find themselves back in prison not long after they are released. If they have no one to mentor them, guide them, or help them, they will fail. Someone has to be clever enough to set them straight and get them settled. How many felons have educated, informed people in their lives? It is virtually impossible to do this without a competent person with some financial means to help the felon. There is little to no way they will succeed on their own. But that's another book that needs to be written.

While I do not wish to go into the extensive details of what I had to do to help this kid once he was released, I do wish to share one remarkable occurrence that needs to be mentioned. Never give up thinking that there are no good people left. There are many people who want to help others. You need to be the advocate to let them know how to help. Angels appear when necessary. And believe me, the few angels I have encountered look nothing like you'd think.

When I knew he was going to be released, I literally wrote to every manufacturer in the city. It was the same letter to every owner of a company, totaling about fifty businesses. I simply explained my situation. I wrote that this young man would be released from prison soon. He needed a job. He had no skills or training. Basically, I pleaded to their humanitarian side to ask if they could find any job for this kid to get him started. It was a huge gamble. I also mentioned that he was Black, and I was his single, white mother who had adopted him at age eight. It was important that they know these facts. This is the Deep South. Things like this matter.

I heard back from no one for three weeks. Nothing. I knew it was a gamble, but I believed it was worth a try. Then one evening, I received a phone message from a man. His voice was gruff and to the point. He said he owned the Rubber & Gasket Company in town. He told me to bring my son to see him when he was released and that I must accompany him. He was a man of few words. But it absolutely made my day. I had a glimmer of hope that maybe someone could help get him started. The funny thing is, when I closed my eyes that night, I remember thinking, *What the hell is a gasket?*

When my son got home from prison, I bought him a jacket, tie, dress shirt, and trousers from a consignment store. He looked appropriate. We went to meet this man. This owner was a big, rough, burly guy in his seventies. He would be what people in the South call a "good ol' boy." He sat us down, looked directly at my son, and asked him why he should give him a job. He actually told my son that he had fifty employees and not one of them was Black. He asked him if he'd have an issue with being the only Black worker. Then he said to him, "What could you possibly do to help my business?"

Finally, it was time for my son to speak. Believe me, we had practiced speaking proper English, using proper manners, shaking hands, etc. This young man who hadn't seen the outside of a prison for eight and a half years looked directly at this man. He opened his mouth and with beautiful, proper English, he spoke. "Sir, skin color is not an issue for me, as you will notice my mom. I do not have much training, but I'm a good listener and a hard worker. I am strong and can run fast. I hope that you will give me a chance."

There was dead silence. My eyes were watering. The owner looked at me out of the corner of his eye. I believe he was giving me affirmation to what was just said. Then the owner looked at him and said, "I am in my seventies. I have not done a lot for others unless they were my own kids. But before I retire, I would like to do one nice thing. You, young man, owe it to your mom for reaching out to help you. That tells me that if she is your mom, your heart is the same. I realize you have been lost for far too long. It's now time for you to prove your worth. Show up here on Monday and you will work eight hours a day, checking rubber tires for leaks. I will pay you $20 an hour. In six months, we will have a meeting to see how this has worked out for you and me. Don't be late." This lost boy sat there with the biggest grin and simply said, "Thank you, sir."

There was so much to do to get him ready for work. He no longer had a driver's license or a Social Security card. Over the last decade, those items were long gone. Therefore, he had no identification cards or anything to prove who he was. All I had was his birth certificate, and I knew his Social Security number because I'd applied for it when I'd adopted him at age eight.

We went to the Social Security Administration Office and took a number. Seventy minutes later, we were called. I explained the whole situation to the clerk and gave him the Social Security number. All we wanted was a duplicate card. The clerk looked us and said he could not help us without proper identification. He instructed us to go to the DMV to get an ID card, even if he didn't have a driver's license. So, we drove across town to the DMV. As always, it was crowded. We took a number and waited another hour. By this time, I was getting impatient.

Finally, our number appeared on the screen. We politely went to the counter, and I slowly and clearly explained that we needed an ID card for my son. The clerk looked at us and told us he couldn't get an ID card without a Social Security card. Then she told us to go to the Social Security office. I tried to reason with her, for I had his birth certificate. Nothing. I am a gentle person, but I would truly have loved to punch someone at this point.

We returned to the Social Security office to wait another hour. We asked for the same clerk, so we waited an additional fifteen minutes.

When we finally got his attention, I was almost in tears, explaining this Catch 22 and asking what we were going to do now. I will never forget how he helped us solve this dilemma. The solution was totally unorthodox and made no sense; however, we were tired and desperate now. (Reminder: What newly released felon could do all of this on his/her own with no help or support?)

The clerk scribbled down an address of a shelter in the rough part of town. He instructed me to drive there with my son. There was a doctor who worked for free at this shelter. The doctor didn't ask a lot of questions. He simply viewed his medical work as a mission. The clerk said if we were lucky enough to be there when the doctor was working, he'd help us. He told us that the doctor would examine my son and write him a prescription with my son's full name on the prescription. Then all I had to do was return him to the Social Security office with the prescription and he'd reissue a Social Security card for him. It made no logical sense to me, but we had no other choice.

I took the address from him. It was in a really rough part of town. It took us a while to find it. Finally, we knocked on the dark, dreary door. No response. So, discouraged, we knocked again. As if the universe felt like we needed a break, the door opened. There stood a young, tall doctor with a stethoscope around his neck. He greeted us kindly but said he was just leaving for his job at the hospital. I worked fast. I poured out our whole story with all my heart.

He looked at his watch and said he had a few minutes. He took my son back to his medical room. I waited anxiously. After a while, the doctor returned to tell me that my son had a serious case of psoriasis and eczema on his head. I had known his head looked awful, dry, and scabby. The doctor wrote him a prescription with his entire name on it and asked that he return in a week or so to see if it improved. He didn't charge us a dime. I hugged this young man so hard. He simply told me that because he'd been given much, he wanted to give back.

We literally ran through red lights to return to the Social Security office before it closed. We walked in and found the clerk. He smiled at us as he took the prescription. Within fifteen minutes, we had his new Social Security card. Finally. I'll never understand that process, but my lips are zipped.

His driver's license was long gone too. It had been ten years since he'd received his first license. Therefore, he had to start all over by taking the written test and the driving test. If you have been driving for years, you probably have no idea how difficult the written test is. We take driving for granted, but I would bet few of us know all of the small details and rules.

I had to help him get a license so he could drive to work each day. I found practice tests online. The problem was that he was very limited in his reading ability. So, I literally sat with him for hours, taking these practice tests. I'd read the question, and we'd try to figure out the answer. To be perfectly honest, we initially failed miserably. We continued to practice for hours and hours. I was learning as much as he was.

I remember getting impatient with him if he yawned or looked bored. He *had* to get a driver's license. The last thing I wanted to do all weekend was to sit in front of this computer. The problem was, even if he finally memorized the answers, how was he going to read the test on his own? His reading ability was very limited.

Finally, after an entire weekend of sitting in front of the computer making him practice, we went to the DMV on Monday morning. I was not worried about the driving part of the test. Physically, he was an incredible driver, far better than my other two kids. He was naturally gifted in anything that required hand-eye coordination.

I purposely chose a rural DMV, thinking there would be less people and he'd be more relaxed. I was right—the place was not busy. I went to the counter and quietly explained that my son needed to take the test after ten years of being imprisoned. I whispered to her that I was concerned that he'd have trouble reading the questions (which I personally felt should be a prerequisite for driving a car. But hey, I had to get this kid started, so I kept that thought to myself). To my very pleasant surprise, the clerk said that was no problem. With earphones, the test would be read to him orally. What a relief! I almost hugged her.

So off he went to listen to the exam. He passed it with a score of 80 percent, enough to get his license. Then the driving part was truly a piece of cake for him. It was one of the happiest days I'd had in a long time. This was a day that began his independence.

Time went on and finally he was getting settled. The job was going well. It was mundane, hot, and exhausting, but he never complained. I had found him an old truck to get him back and forth to work and was looking into finding him his own apartment. He had been staying with me. I had a lovely, but tiny, condo. He took over my loft, temporarily. However, the neighbors in this high-end community stared when they'd see a young Black man coming and going from my one-bedroom condo. It was causing a stir.

It was exhausting on my part, trying to balance my life and getting his started. The nosy neighbors didn't help. One day I finally marched him over to the worst offender and introduced my son to her. She was in shock as she looked at this young Black man. Then my son added, "If I can be of any help to you around your yard, I'm willing to do whatever you need. I'm great with a lawn mower." Fortunately, after that introduction, word spread like wildfire, and the stares stopped.

There was only one incident that might be worth mentioning. One evening after he came home from work, he was dirty and sweaty and parked in the front of my small condo. He had been trying to put a radio in the old truck. Finally, he got it to work. He yelled excitedly to me to come see. He was thrilled as I came running out of my condo in my bare feet to see his victory. We both had our heads in the truck listening to his music. All of a sudden, a police car pulled up next to us. We didn't even see him. The police officer walked over to us. He asked me if I was in any danger and if there was trouble here. I looked at him in shock. Then I introduced my son to him and thanked him for stopping by to check on *us*. It was humiliating, and I will never forget how that must have made my son feel. He nonchalantly shrugged it off, for he'd had a lifetime of such episodes. Prejudice is hurtful on so many levels.

Each day he was becoming more comfortable with being a free citizen. I could see the life coming back into his eyes. He didn't look as scared anymore. His personality slowly returned. He'd always been on the quiet side, but at least now he could converse once again. He no longer spoke in his prison manner. He used proper English.

I was able to get him an apartment for a reasonable amount. He understood that I expected him to keep up with the rent and utilities. I helped him with the initial security deposit and furniture. I had many friends that gave him almost everything he'd need to establish an apartment. At almost twenty-nine years old, he was finally independent. Of course, he continued to call daily for advice on various issues. It absolutely amazed me at how little he knew about how things worked in the world, especially when it came to technology. I will never forget the first time I taught him to use an ATM. He was very intimidated by the whole process. Nothing like living in a vacuum for almost a decade.

Unhappily for me, he eventually befriended the same eleven guys and his former girlfriend who had abandoned him ten years earlier. The thought of him going back to them frightened me. I tried to discourage his choice to reunite with them. But being desperate for friends, he ignored my plea. He went right back to them. I just shook my head silently. Fortunately, most of them had graduated from college by now and matured into decent adults. In fact, several invited him to join their active churches. I tried to quit worrying and let him move on with his life. I totally understood his need to have friends. He had discovered religion while in prison and it seemed to help him to survive the last few years of his imprisonment. I figured that as long as they were all involved in a church, it would be OK. They truly embraced him and invited him into their adult lives.

Then he got involved with his former girlfriend. Of course, she and the other boys all profusely apologized to him for abandoning him while he was in prison. He was quick to forgive them. Not me, but I remained quiet. In the meantime, he and his former girlfriend were spending a lot of time together. It's funny how I never knew her from high school, and she never called me over the long years he was away to check on him. I truly had no idea she existed.

One day, she came to him to tell him she was pregnant with another Black man's baby. She was white. When that had happened, the guy abandoned her. She immediately grabbed on tight to my son. I watched this in disbelief. She told him that she'd been in love with him all of these years and wanted to be with him. I just shook my head in silence.

I sat him down and pleaded with him to take another year or so and get his feet on the ground. He still had much more to learn about being a successful adult. I was still helping him with banking accounts, budgets, bills, etc. I told him to take it slowly and that she'd wait for him if she truly loved him. I did not trust her motives, but I did not want to hurt his feelings. However, my gut was telling me that this was not what he should do.

He did not take my advice. He ignored any of my reasoning with him. He moved in with this girl and took on this baby as his own. Since he was Black, no one would question his paternity. I was very disappointed, only because I believed he needed more time. I did not want him to make a rash decision. But who am I to judge? Loneliness is a powerful motivator, even if it's for all the wrong reasons...I had learned that lesson. Within the next year, she was pregnant again with his baby. They secretly went off and got married.

She knew I didn't approve of her motives and could see through what she'd done. She talked poorly of me to him. She disapproved of me trying to reason with him. It was too late. I had to step back. I could do no more to help this man who was now thirty years old. Luckily, her parents were very happy that their daughter, with few suitors, had found someone to love her. Her parents embraced this union and brought all four of them into their home. Now he finally had the family he always dreamed of having. There was no more need for my help. He became toxic toward me because I had not blessed this marriage and did not feel close to their babies. In time, they dismissed me from their life. They now had what they needed and didn't want me to be part of any of it.

You would have thought I'd be terribly hurt and angry. I probably should have been, knowing the twenty years of giving, sacrifice, and heartache I had experienced. But I must be honest in saying that when they dismissed me, I was extremely relieved. Secretly, I wanted them to go on and leave me alone. I was so tired. I had given and sacrificed so much for him. Now it was finally over. I was finally done. Yet it is just so ironic that I became the villain in the scenario. However, I'm wise enough to understand that this happens. Someone has to take the blame and maybe I had been wrong not to embrace his new life. But I just couldn't. My faith is strong enough to understand why it happened this way. The universe allowed me to send him on his way now, without my help anymore. He was now a man, a husband and a father. My job was done. Maybe, just maybe, all those years of pain and sacrifice did pay off after all. I have not heard from him in years now, but I pray for him daily and hope his life has continued to flourish. I pray that he has everything he ever wanted out of life.

In the meantime, my older son was excelling in the military. After his deployment in Iraq, he had the opportunity to stay with the Army as a reservist and was accepted into a four-year internship program to be trained to be a lineman/journeyman for the state's electric company. He continued to serve in the reserves and worked as an apprentice for four years. He graduated first in his class. I had always known he was a bright guy. He just had to find his way. He also met the girl of his dreams. They married, and I could not have been happier for them. He was absolutely soaring. He had matured into an amazing soldier, successful lineman, happy homeowner, and loving husband. To see this transformation from a lost teen to a true hero was the biggest joy of my life. He would go on to spend a second year in a dangerous place in the Middle East. While on this second deployment, he was a strong soldier and brave leader to his younger men of which he led while in this frightening place. I could not be prouder of him, whom I view as a true American hero.

My daughter started her own law practice out west after a few years of working for other attorneys. She was killing it on her own. This beautiful, smart young woman could do anything. I have always been her biggest fan. She met a wonderful man and they married. Both were very successful in their chosen professions. They have a storybook life on a gorgeous, big farm with lots of animals. Then they gave me the two most precious gifts of my life: two little granddaughters. It took almost thirty-seven years for my daughter to see the truth about her mother. Maybe it took her to become a mother to see how deep my love had always been for her and just how much I truly cared about her journey. I attribute it to God's hand that her view of me has completely changed. She sees me now as a woman who never gave up and never stopped seeing the world through the eyes of love.

I wanted to mention that although their father and I did not have a successful marriage, we have remained life-long partners in raising these two kids. He has always been supportive of my decisions concerning the kids, my guidance, my parenting style, and my discipline. Our two kids knew that they had two parents who were partners in raising them. They knew we were a united front. To this day, their father is my friend. I know that if I ever needed anything in this world, he would be there without hesitation.

Note to self: Perhaps things didn't work out exactly how one hopes, but they worked out how they should.

Chapter Thirty

ALMOST SIXTY YEARS OF MY LIFE HAS PASSED BY NOW. I CAN'T say that I'd want to relive a minute of it. But I can say that I have never given up on my belief that a higher power has guided me through the hell I have lived. I have never stopped thanking the universe for my blessings and guidance. My kids are all fine now and living the lives that they chose. I am on the top of my game as a veteran teacher with retirement staring me in the eye. I have special friends, good health, a caring heart, and a pretty face. I'm truly grateful and expect nothing more.

But then the best miracle of my life happened. At fifty-nine years old, I was walking the beach as I did almost daily. It was not only great exercise, but it was also therapy for my tired mind. I was entering my last year as an educator. It was my thirty-fifth year in the classroom. Even though I wasn't sure I'd be able to totally retire due to the small pension teachers earned, at least I'd be able to do something less grueling and more mindless. It was fun just thinking about what lay ahead for me. The idea of working in a beautiful Charleston B&B or a fancy-dress shop sounded delightful.

There is a particular beach in the Charleston area where surfers frequent. It's fun to watch them as I've never been on a surfboard. It must feel extremely freeing. They make it look easy as they glide on the waves. To do something beautiful with only one piece of equipment seemed like a perfect sport to me. A bathing suit and a surfboard was all that was needed. As I was walking by, a man was resting next to his board. He was wearing a black wet suit since the water was cold in December. It was obvious that he was a seasoned surfer. He smiled and commented on the lovely winter weather. I took that as an invitation to stop for a moment to chat. I asked him about surfing and his history. It turned out that this man, at the age of sixty-three, had been surfing for fifty-three years. He started in Miami at the age of ten and had never stopped. He said that nothing made him happier than when he is riding a wave alone. He explained that this particular beach left a lot to be desired as far as its waves, but he had just been transferred here from Florida with his company, and if he wanted to surf, this was the best it was going to get. We chatted for a while, and my first impression of him was that he was a man that seemed gentle, kind, and humble. However, I've been fooled before, more times than I can count. So, I just enjoyed the moment of light conversation. I was secretly admiring his weathered face, his longer hair, and his tight physique. Why is it that older men look so attractive with wrinkled, leathery skin, yet we women are not as lucky? It doesn't seem fair.

As I was about to continue my power walk, he asked me if he could show me something funny. He grabbed his board, ran into the ocean, and paddled out. I saw him sit up on his board, but then right before my eyes, he did a head stand on his board as he rode the waves in toward me. I was amazed, actually astonished! Who does that? Who can surf on their head? I was clapping and laughing with joy.

He walked toward me and said that it's no big deal that any monkey can do it. I laughed and told him I should ask him for his autograph. I asked him if he does this for all the girls walking by him on the beach. He winked and said, "Only the hot ones!" This made me laugh out loud.

Then he shyly asked me if I might like to have a coffee or a drink with him. He was new here and had no idea where to go for a nice drink. He told me I was about the first human he'd had a conversation with since he moved here. He said he was not happy about the transfer and had kept himself busy surfing to forget his disappointment. I was secretly smiling ear to ear as I told him that I have just the place for a lovely glass of wine.

We met for that drink. It was the most perfect date I'd ever had. We shared our stories for hours. He was also single and had been married to an alcoholic. His marriage was very difficult, and his ex-wife was terribly mean when she drank, which was a daily occurrence. He stayed in the marriage in order to raise his precious daughters with two parents intact. But the moment his daughters were raised, he filed for a divorce. He finally was free from a very difficult twenty-five years. It appeared that neither of us had had an easy fifty-plus years. We were both entering that twilight phase of life, and both of us shared a great relief to now be living without family drama.

He told me that his dream had always been to live in Hawaii, specifically Maui, where the waves never end. But he followed the conventional route of going to college, getting married, raising children, and working to support the family. His dream was now only a dream and it sort of passed by with never coming to fruition. But he had long ago come to terms with it being nothing more than a childhood daydream.

From that first date, we both felt the magic. It continued, and our excitement to be together never dulled. After that lovely first drink, we were never apart. We spent every minute together. I had not known such happiness. He was not only handsome, but he was also smart and attentive. He had a nice job and made a nice living.

A year later, he and I secretly went off to the courthouse and got married. He felt strongly about us being married. He loved the idea of being a spiritually united couple. I agreed. We were blissfully happy. However, I was careful not to share this news with my brothers or those judgmental friends that I had come to realize enjoyed using my unconventional life as a subject of their gossip.

The fact that this was my fourth marriage was not something I was proud to claim. Life just seemed to happen that way for me. This darling man never cared for a minute that I'd had multiple marriages. He just kissed me and told me it was because I was so lovable, and everyone wanted me. I was truly relieved that he loved me regardless of the past. We kept our union quiet and just wanted to float along in this blissful state of joy. I figured that those who truly loved me, unconditionally, would find out that we married and be happy for us, without judgement. No need to give others something to use for their gossip sessions. And this is exactly what happened. True friends celebrated with us. They danced at our celebration party six months later. They were genuinely happy for us. And guess what? My two brothers showed up and held up their glasses in our honor.

It is important to mention, that God blessed me with a special bonus, something I had longed for all of my life. My husband has a mother who, although she is in her 90s, is independent, brilliant, computer savvy, generous, accepting of others, and probably the wisest woman I've ever known. If I was to list a dream mother figure, she would be the exact woman I would hope to have in my life. She has taught me many things as I have watched her view the world. Not only his mom, but he has two older sisters who have accepted me as their little sister. All three of these ladies have given me what I have only dreamed of having for over sixty years. It is another dream come true for me.

Shortly thereafter, I retired from teaching. It was a beautiful ending to a long career. I will believe until the day I die that I was excellent at two very important jobs in my life: being an educator and being a mother. While other areas in my life might not have been as successful, I have never doubted how hard I tried to teach and love every single child that the universe placed in my path.

One lazy Sunday after we retired, I looked at my prince and said, "Let's make your dream happen! It's time for us to fulfill our dreams. It's time for us to do what we'd like to do. We needn't have to care for anyone else anymore. It's our time now. Let's move to Maui!"

He stared at me in disbelief. He got teary-eyed and couldn't speak. He hugged me and seemed dazed by my idea. He looked at me as if to say, *how?*

I saw him at his computer the next day. He had our budget pulled up on the screen and was crunching the numbers in every way possible. We both knew we were living on pensions now and that Maui was extremely expensive in every area. But we put our heads together and looked closely at the numbers. We figured we could do it if we lived simply and smart. Fingers crossed.

We flew to Maui for a week. We fell in love with the island. We bought a small condo on the ocean during that visit. It was totally spontaneous and exciting, probably the most exciting thing the two of us have ever done in the six decades we have lived thus far. This small, sweet condo had the most spectacular view one could ever dream of seeing. The ocean was directly in front of our condo with the islands of Lanai and Moloka'i in perfect view. Truly the prettiest view I'd ever experienced.

We returned to Charleston and sold our home and everything we owned. We packed clothes and a few important sentimental items and